THE BEST OF
COOK'S
MAGAZINE

Edited by
Judith Hill
and
Kathryn Knapp

Pennington Publishing, Inc.

Published by Pennington Publishing Inc.
2710 North Avenue
Bridgeport, Connecticut 06604

ISBN: 0-936599-08-1

The Best of Cook's Magazine Cookbook / edited by Judith Hill and
Kathryn Knapp.
    p.   cm.
  Includes index.
  ISBN 0-936559-08-1
    1. Cookery. I. Hill, Judith, 1945-   . II. Knapp, Kathryn,
1959-   . III. Cook's magazine.
TX715.B485553 1987
641.5 – bc19   87-25834

Contents

Introduction

The Best of COOK'S Magazine is just that. We've chosen our favorite recipes for this book—the recipes from the last eight years that we like the best, refer to most often, and continue to make ourselves. They include down-home recipes, such as the perfect Old-Fashioned Fried Chicken, and new ideas, such as Thyme Crêpes with Chanterelles and Veal. They span the menu from clever hors d'oeuvre, such as Cornbread Canapés with Ham and Maple Butter, to luscious desserts like Caramel Pecan Tartlets. They range from simple recipes, like Trout with Herb Butter Sauce, that first appeared in our "Quick From Scratch" column to an elaborate production like pastry chef Albert Kumin's Chocolate Meringue Cake, the most glorious chocolate cake we've ever put in our mouths. Most of the recipes, of course, reflect COOK'S predominant style—simple but sophisticated, up to date yet firmly based in traditional cooking.

A Word about the Recipes

Our recipes are divided, as a rule, into PREPARATION and COOKING AND SERVING sections. Under PREPARATION, you will find all the steps that can be completed at least an hour ahead, and very often farther in advance. These steps may well include some preliminary cooking, and sometimes, as in a cake recipe for instance, all the cooking and finishing may be done ahead of time and therefore will fall in the PREPARATION section. In such cases, the second section is called simply SERVING. For every recipe in this book, you have only to look at the second section, be it COOKING AND SERVING or just SERVING, to know exactly how much work is involved just before the dish is taken to the table.

Christopher Kimball
Publisher

Judith Hill
Editor in Chief

Acknowledgments

We would like to thank, first and foremost, all of the cooks who have contributed recipes over the years to the magazine and therefore to this book. Our thanks go as well to Kathryn Knapp, who co-edited the book, to Lee Buccino, Donna Pintek, and Sally Williams, all of whom helped in the editing, and to the editors of the magazine, Lisa Carlson, Sheila Lowenstein, and Pamela Parseghian.

We are greatful to COOK'S art director, Leith Harbold, who designed the book, and to her associate art director, Cara Formisano. Sara Barbaris directed all of the beautiful photography, and Beverly Cox styled the food for many of the pictures. We thank both of them and our illustrator, Marty Schwartz.

Christopher Kimball
Publisher

Judith Hill
Editor in Chief

HORS
D'OEUVRE
AND FIRST
COURSES

Cornbread Canapés with Ham and Maple Butter

RICHARD FELBER

This all-American hors d'oeuvre with its cornbread and maple butter is appropriate any time of the year.

INGREDIENTS

Cornbread

2	cups yellow cornmeal
½	cup flour
2	teaspoons baking powder
1	teaspoon salt
½	teaspoon baking soda
4	tablespoons butter
1	cup buttermilk
1	cup milk
2	eggs

Maple Butter

6	ounces softened butter
1	tablespoon maple syrup
½	teaspoon Dijon mustard
12	thin slices smoked ham
1	ear corn *or* ½ cup frozen corn
¼	cup chopped fresh parsley
1	tablespoon coarse black pepper

METHOD

PREPARATION: *For the cornbread,* heat oven to 450°F. Butter a 12- by 18-inch baking pan. Combine the dry ingredients in a large bowl. Melt the butter. Mix together the melted butter, buttermilk, milk, and eggs. Combine with the dry ingredients.

Pour mixture into prepared pan and bake in preheated oven until cornbread shrinks from sides of pan, 10 to 15 minutes. Cool bread in the pan.

Then turn onto a baking sheet. Using a long, serrated knife, trim to an even ⅜-inch thickness.

For the Maple Butter, combine the softened butter, maple syrup, and mustard. Spread on the cornbread. Cover with the ham slices and refrigerate.

Cook the ear of corn in boiling, salted water until tender. Cut kernels from ear. Or blanch the frozen corn kernels in boiling, salted water. Drain.

Chop the parsley. Using a 1½-inch round pastry cutter, cut out the canapés.

Canapés can be made several hours ahead and refrigerated.

SERVING: Return canapés to room temperature before serving. Garnish each canapé with parsley, a generous sprinkling of black pepper, and the corn.

YIELD: 32 canapés

For the Cornbread Canapés, spread Maple Butter over surface of trimmed cornbread.

Lay ham on top of Maple Butter. Chill to harden butter and cut out with 1½-inch pastry cutter.

Salmon-Butter Triangles with Caviar and Dill

RICHARD FELBER

A splash of vodka adds to the already welcome combination of salmon and caviar.

INGREDIENTS

4	ounces smoked salmon
¼	pound softened butter
2	teaspoons chopped fresh dill *or*
½	teaspoon dried dill
2	teaspoons vodka
	Pepper
8	thin slices white bread
1	ounce American golden caviar
	Sprigs fresh dill for garnish

METHOD

PREPARATION: In a food processor, puree salmon, gradually adding the butter until well combined. Add dill, vodka, and pepper to taste. Process until incorporated. Chill slightly before spreading.

Spread each slice of bread evenly with salmon butter. Trim off crusts and cut each slice into 4 triangles.

Canapés can be made to this point several hours ahead. Cover well and refrigerate.

SERVING: Return canapés to room temperature before serving. Garnish each triangle with caviar and a small sprig of dill.

YIELD: 32 canapés

Crab Canapés with Citrus Butter

Fresh ingredients, balanced flavors, and modern design result in eye-catching canapés.

RICHARD FELBER

INGREDIENTS

Citrus Butter

1	green onion
1	tablespoon minced fresh ginger
1	lemon
2	limes
¼	pound softened butter
	Salt

8 thin slices white bread
6 ounces fresh crabmeat

METHOD

PREPARATION: *For the Citrus Butter,* chop 1 tablespoon onion. Mince the ginger. Grate 1 tablespoon zest from the lemon. Squeeze 1 teaspoon juice. Grate 2 teaspoons zest from one of the limes. Squeeze 1 tablespoon juice. Cut thin slices from the second lime. Cut 48 tiny wedges from the slices and reserve for garnish.

In a bowl, combine butter, onion, ginger, lemon and lime zests, lemon and lime juices, and salt to taste until thoroughly incorporated. Spread each slice of bread with about 1 tablespoon Citrus Butter. Trim edges and cut each slice into 6 rectangular pieces, first cutting bread into thirds and then cutting each third in half.

Canapés can be made to this point several hours ahead. Wrap well and refrigerate.

SERVING: Bring canapés to room temperature before serving. Put a small portion of crabmeat on top of each buttered rectangle. Garnish with a small wedge of lime.

YIELD: 48 canapés

Blue-Cheese Triangles with Toasted Hazelnuts

Pungent blue cheese, full-flavored whole wheat, and crunchy hazelnuts give earthy appeal to this canapé.

RICHARD FELBER

INGREDIENTS

2	ounces hazelnuts (about ½ cup)
¼	pound softened butter
3	ounces room-temperature blue cheese
8	thin slices whole-wheat bread

METHOD

PREPARATION: Heat oven to 350°F. Spread hazelnuts on a baking sheet in a single layer and toast until browned, stirring once or twice, about 10 minutes. Cool, rub off loose skins, and chop. Set aside.

In a bowl, cream the butter and blue cheese together. Spread each slice of bread evenly with the mixture. Cut off the crusts and cut each slice into 4 even triangles.

Canapés can be made to this point several hours ahead. Cover well and refrigerate.

SERVING: Bring to room temperature before serving. Garnish canapés with the hazelnuts.

YIELD: 32 canapés

REFRIGERATING CANAPÉS

If you want to make canapés several hours before serving, allow plenty of refrigerator space for your trays or baking sheets. Use toothpicks at each corner as stilts to hold the plastic wrap above the canapés. Take out of the refrigerator 15 to 30 minutes before serving to let flavors "warm up."

Recipes on these 2 pages by:
Susy Davidson
Director of Membership and
   Chapter Development
American Institute of Wine
   and Food
San Francisco, CA

Shrimp and Guacamole Tostadas

These hors d'oeuvre combine cool shrimp and hot jalapenos, crunchy chips and smooth guacamole.

INGREDIENTS

Lime-Coriander Marinade
1 lime
1 tablespoon chopped coriander
1 small clove garlic
¼ cup oil
1 teaspoon Dijon mustard
¼ teaspoon ground cumin
Salt and pepper

12 shrimp, in the shell

Guacamole
1 plum tomato
1 fresh or pickled jalapeno pepper
1 lime
2 ripe avocados
Salt and pepper

24 round corn tortilla chips
Coriander sprigs for garnish

METHOD

PREPARATION: *For the Lime-Coriander Marinade,* squeeze 2 tablespoons juice from the lime. Chop the coriander. Crush the garlic. Combine the lime juice, coriander, garlic, oil, mustard, cumin, and salt and pepper to taste.

In a pot of boiling, salted water, cook the shrimp until they turn pink, about 2 minutes. Drain, cool enough to handle, and shell the shrimp. Cut in half lengthwise through the back and devein. Combine warm shrimp with marinade, cool to room temperature, and refrigerate at least 1 hour.

For the Guacamole, peel, seed, and mince the tomato. Seed and mince the jalapeno. Squeeze 2 tablespoons juice from the lime. Peel the avocados. In a bowl, mash the avocados with a fork or potato masher. They shouldn't be perfectly smooth. Combine avocados, tomato, jalapeno, lime juice, and salt and pepper to taste. If not using immediately, press plastic wrap directly on surface of guacamole and refrigerate.

Recipe can be completed to this point several hours ahead.

SERVING: Heat oven to 350°F. Put corn chips on a baking sheet and heat in oven until they are crisp and golden, about 5 minutes. Cool slightly. Drain shrimp. Put about 2 teaspoons of the guacamole on each corn chip. Put a shrimp half, cut side down, on top of guacamole. Garnish each with a small sprig of coriander.

YIELD: 24 tostadas

Brooke Dojny
Free-lance writer
Westport, CT

Fried Red-Onion Rings

Sweet summer onions and just a dusting of flour make these onion rings more delicate and flavorful than the usual batter-dipped ones.

INGREDIENTS

3 **large red onions**
1 **quart milk**
2 **cups flour**
   Salt and pepper
   Peanut oil for frying

METHOD

PREPARATION: Cut the onions into ¼-inch slices and separate into rings. Put onions in a nonreactive bowl, cover with milk, and let soak for at least 30 minutes. Mix together the flour, 1 teaspoon salt, and ½ teaspoon pepper.

Recipe can be completed to this point about 1 hour ahead.

COOKING AND SERVING: In a deep-fryer or large, heavy frying pan, heat about an inch of oil to 375°F. Dredge the onion rings in the flour mixture and fry a few at a time until golden, about 3 minutes. Drain on paper towels.

Put the onion rings directly on plates or napkins or on a serving platter. Do not pile in a basket or cover or the onion rings will become soggy. Serve immediately.

YIELD: 4 servings

Alice Waters
Owner
Chez Panisse and
   Café Fanny
Berkeley, CA

Smoked-Sausage Brioche

RICHARD FELBER

The addition of smoked sausage turns classic buttery brioche into a splendid hors d'oeuvre.

INGREDIENTS

Brioche Dough

 5 **eggs**
 1 **tablespoon yeast**
 2 **tablespoons lukewarm water**
 2 **teaspoons sugar**
 6 **ounces butter**
 2 **cups flour**
 2 **teaspoons salt**

 ½ **pound smoked garlic sausage**

METHOD

PREPARATION: *For the dough,* bring 4 of the eggs to room temperature. Warm in hot water (in the shell), if time is short. Butter a large bowl.

In a small bowl, mix yeast with 2 tablespoons lukewarm water and the sugar. Set aside for 10 minutes.

To make brioche using a standing mixer or food processor, melt the butter over low heat and allow to cool slightly. In the bowl of a standing electric mixer fitted with dough hook or in a food processor fitted with the plastic blade, combine the flour and salt. Whisk together the 4 room-temperature eggs. With machine running, add eggs to the flour. Beat mixture until eggs are thoroughly incorporated, about 2 minutes in mixer, 8 seconds in a food processor. Add the dissolved yeast mixture and beat to combine. With machine running, slowly add the tepid butter. Mix on medium speed for another 5 minutes if using an electric mixer, 15 seconds in a food processor, scraping the sides of the bowl if

12

necessary. The dough should be sticky and should pull away from the sides of the bowl.

To make brioche by hand, be sure butter is thoroughly chilled. Sift the flour onto a cool work surface and make a large well in the center. Whisk the 4 room-temperature eggs and put in the center of the well. Add yeast mixture and salt to the well. With your fingers, combine the salt, eggs, and yeast. Draw in the remaining wall of flour using both hands, lightly working the mixture with your fingertips until it forms large crumbs.

Knead the dough by grasping it from underneath with both hands and then forcefully throwing it back down onto the work surface, at the same time pulling fingers away from the dough. Continue this process for about 10 minutes until dough is very smooth and elastic.

Pound the cold butter with a rolling pin, fold it in half, and repeat pounding and folding until it is soft and workable but still cold. Break the softened butter into small pieces. Work into the dough a portion at a time by smearing the dough and butter together with the heel of your hand, frequently using a pastry scraper or spatula to pull the dough back together and to chop the butter into smaller bits. Do this until butter is well mixed into the dough. If the dough is too loose to knead at this point, refrigerate until it firms up. Finish the dough by kneading again, as above, for a couple of minutes.

After dough has been made by mixer, food processor, or by hand, dust the dough very lightly with flour, transfer to the buttered bowl, and turn to coat surface with butter. Cover the bowl with a damp cloth and let stand in a warm place to rise until dough is nearly doubled in bulk, about 2 hours.

Once dough has risen, put it on a lightly floured work surface and fold in thirds to deflate. Put dough back in the bowl, cover with a damp cloth, and let stand to rise a second time, either in a warm place or overnight in the refrigerator, until doubled in bulk.

Chill dough thoroughly before shaping. Meanwhile, butter a 6-inch brioche mold. Cut the sausage lengthwise into quarters and then into thin slices.

Fold the dough to deflate. Sprinkle sausage slices over brioche and fold over and over again to gently but thoroughly incorporate sausage.

Twist off ¼ of the dough and roll both large and small pieces into balls. Put the large ball in prepared mold. With a small, sharp knife, cut a deep cross in the top of the large ball and put the small ball into it. Let the shaped brioche rise in a warm place until the pan is almost full, about 1 hour.

Heat oven to 425°F. Beat remaining egg and brush a light coating of it over the brioche. Bake in preheated oven until well browned, about 15 minutes. Lower heat to 375°F and continue baking until it pulls away from the sides of the mold, about 30 more minutes. If at any point the brioche threatens to brown too much, cover it loosely with foil and continue to bake. Remove from oven and cool.

The brioche can be served on the day it is baked or can be made a day ahead and freshened by heating in a 325°F oven for 10 minutes.

SERVING: Cut loaf into thin wedges and then cut each wedge in half.

YIELD: one 6-inch brioche

For the Brioche, *beat the dough until it pulls away from the sides of the bowl and adheres to the paddle or beaters.*

Put the large ball of dough into the brioche pan and cut a cross in the center. Nestle the smaller ball of dough into the cross.

Coriander Quesadillas

Delectable quesadillas get a lift from fresh coriander.

INGREDIENTS

Cornmeal Tortillas
- 1 tablespoon minced fresh coriander
- 1½ cups flour
- ½ cup cornmeal
- 1 teaspoon salt
- 2 tablespoons vegetable shortening
- ½ cup warm water
- Butter and oil for frying

Cheese Filling
- 2 ounces Monterey Jack cheese (about ½ cup shredded)
- 2 ounces sharp cheddar cheese (about ½ cup shredded)
- 2 ounces whole-milk mozzarella cheese (about ½ cup shredded)
- ½ ounce Parmesan cheese (about 2 tablespoons grated)
- ½ teaspoon ground cumin
- Salt
- 4 scallions
- 3 tablespoons minced fresh coriander

Jalapeno pepper for garnish, optional
Sour cream for serving
Fresh coriander sprigs for garnish, optional

METHOD

PREPARATION: *For the tortillas,* mince the coriander. Sift the flour. Combine flour, cornmeal, salt, and coriander in a mixing bowl and cut in shortening until mixture resembles coarse crumbs. Add water and stir until mixture comes together in a ball. Cover with plastic wrap and let rest 2 hours. Divide into 8 balls and roll into thin 7½- to 8-inch circles. If not using immediately, stack with plastic wrap between each layer and wrap well.

Tortillas can be completed several days ahead.

For the filling, shred Monterey Jack, cheddar, and mozzarella cheeses. Grate the Parmesan. Mix the cheeses, cumin, and ½ teaspoon salt together. Mince the scallions, including half of the green part, and coriander and combine them with the cheese mixture.

Cut jalapeno pepper into thin slices if using.

Recipe can be completed to this point 1 hour ahead.

COOKING AND SERVING: Heat 2 large frying pans or a griddle over medium-high heat. Add about 2 teaspoons each of butter and oil to prevent quesadillas from sticking. Put 2 tortilla rounds in each frying pan and put ¼ of the filling on each tortilla. Cover each with another round and press edges together. Cook, turning once, until quesadillas begin to brown, about 3 minutes total.

Serve quesadillas whole or cut into wedges and garnish with sour cream, jalapeno pepper slices, and coriander sprigs if desired.

YIELD: 4 servings

Anne Byrn
Food editor and restaurant
 critic
The Atlanta Journal and *The Atlanta Constitution*

14

Savoy-Cabbage Shrimp Rolls

Delicate Shrimp Mousseline is wrapped up beautifully by mild savoy cabbage.

RICHARD FELBER

INGREDIENTS

Chive and Sour Cream Sauce
- **1 cup sour cream**
- **2 teaspoons rice-wine vinegar or white-wine vinegar**
- **Salt and pepper**
- **½ cup minced chives**

- **1 small head savoy cabbage**

Shrimp Mousseline
- **½ cup dry white wine**
- **1 2-inch piece celery**
- **2 to 3 sprigs parsley**
- **¼ lemon**
- **Salt and pepper**
- **½ pound shrimp, in the shell**
- **½ pound sole or flounder fillets**
- **1 tomato**
- **1 shallot**
- **1 teaspoon anchovy paste**
- **1 slice white bread**
- **¼ cup milk**
- **Hot red-pepper sauce**
- **1 egg white**
- **½ cup heavy cream**

METHOD

PREPARATION: *For the Chive and Sour Cream Sauce,* whisk sour cream, vinegar, and salt and pepper to taste until smooth. Mince the chives and stir into sour-cream mixture. Refrigerate for at least 1 hour.

Core the cabbage. Discard thick outer leaves. Carefully cut off 13 or 14 leaves. In a deep pot, cover cabbage leaves with about 1 cup of water. Bring to a simmer, cover, and cook until leaves are soft and pliable, about 20 minutes. Plunge cabbage leaves into cold water, drain, and pat dry. Trim thick base of each rib with a paring knife. Chill.

For the Shrimp Mousseline, boil ¼ cup of the wine, ¾ cup water, the celery, and parsley in a covered saucepan for about 5 minutes. Cut off a strip of zest from the lemon and add to the pot. Squeeze the lemon juice into the pot and add salt and pepper to taste. Add ¼ of the unpeeled shrimp, cover, reduce heat, and simmer for 1 minute. Drain the shrimp and cool enough to handle. Peel, devein, and mince the cooked shrimp. Chill.

Peel, devein, and halve the remaining uncooked shrimp. Cut fish fillets into 1-inch chunks. Peel, seed, and chop the tomato. Drain. Combine the raw shrimp, fish, and tomato and chill.

Chop the shallot. Put the remaining ¼ cup wine and the shallot in a small saucepan and cook over high heat until liquid is reduced, about 2 minutes. Add anchovy paste and stir to melt. Cool and then add to the shrimp and fish mixture. Refrigerate.

Cut crusts from the bread and soak bread in milk for 5 minutes. Squeeze out as much milk as possible and put bread into a food processor. Add the chilled fish mixture and season to taste with hot red-pepper sauce and salt and pepper. Process just to combine. Scrape down sides. With machine running, add the egg white. Scrape down sides again. With machine running, pour in cream and process until just smooth.

Poach 1 teaspoon of this Shrimp Mousseline in simmering water. Taste and adjust seasoning if necessary. Fold the cooked, minced shrimp into mousseline. Chill for 30 minutes.

Spread out cabbage leaves. Divide shrimp filling among 10 of the leaves, putting it near the base. Roll up the leaves, folding in the sides after the first roll. Use extra cooked leaves to patch where necesssary.

Recipe can be prepared to this point several hours ahead.

COOKING AND SERVING: Bring Chive and Sour Cream Sauce to room temperature. Put the shrimp rolls in a steamer or other pan fitted with a rack. Pour boiling water into the steamer, being careful that water does not touch the rack. Cover, return water to a boil, reduce heat, and simmer until rolls feel firm to the touch, 20 to 25 minutes.

Put rolls on warm plates and top with Chive and Sour Cream Sauce.

YIELD: 10 shrimp rolls

Carol Cutler
Food consultant
Time-Life Cookbooks
Washington, DC

Winter-Squash Ravioli

Alice Waters, owner of Chez Panisse and Café Fanny in Berkeley, California, developed these squash-filled ravioli with a topping of sautéed bread crumbs and sage.

INGREDIENTS

1 **recipe Egg Pasta (page 66)**

Squash Filling
2 **pounds winter squash, such as butternut**
Salt and pepper
4 **cloves garlic**
2 to 3 **sprigs fresh thyme**
Olive oil for drizzling
Butter or cream, if necessary

Bread-Crumb Topping
6 **slices white bread**
4 **tablespoons butter**
2 **tablespoons fresh sage leaves**

METHOD

PREPARATION: Make the pasta dough.

For the filling, heat oven to 350°F. Cut squash in half and scoop out the seeds. Salt and pepper the squash, slash the flesh, and put unpeeled garlic cloves and thyme sprigs in the slashes. Drizzle squash with olive oil and put on a baking sheet, cut sides down. Bake in preheated oven until very soft, about 30 minutes. Cool.

Scoop out pulp from squash. Remove garlic cloves from squash flesh. Squeeze garlic cloves from their skins. Put squash and garlic cloves through a food mill. Adjust seasoning with salt and pepper. The puree's texture will vary depending on the variety of squash; it should be thick with no running juices. If using moist-fleshed squash, pour off excess juices. If squash is dry, add a little butter or cream. Chill.

Recipe can be made to this point 1 day ahead.

Roll out the pasta dough as thin as possible. Cut dough into 12- to 18-inch lengths and lay on lightly floured work surface. Fold each section lengthwise, crease, and then unfold. Put a scant teaspoon of chilled filling every 2 inches just under the crease. With a pastry brush dipped in water, moisten pasta around each teaspoon of filling. Fold top half of dough over filling and press firmly around each mound of filling. Flour pasta very lightly. Use a cutter-crimper to cut into ravioli. Or cut with a knife and crimp-cut edges firmly with the tines of a fork. Put ravioli, well spaced, on lightly floured baking sheets or waxed paper. Refrigerate if not cooking immediately.

For the topping, tear the 6 slices of bread into large bread crumbs, about ¾-inch squares.

Recipe can be completed to this point several hours ahead.

COOKING AND SERVING: Cook ravioli in a large pot of boiling, salted water until tender, 5 to 10 minutes. Drain well.

Melt the butter and sauté the bread crumbs until almost golden, about 4 minutes. Add the sage leaves, stirring frequently until the bread crumbs are golden, about 1 minute.

Toss the ravioli with croutons and sage and serve at once.

YIELD: 4 servings

Alice Waters
Owner
Chez Panisse and
    Café Fanny
Berkeley, CA

Sautéed Chicken Wontons

Ordinary chicken puts on the ritz in this unusual, delectable appetizer.

RICHARD FELBER

INGREDIENTS

Chicken-Tamari Filling
- 9 **scallions**
- 5 **ounces boneless chicken thighs**
- 2 **teaspoons tamari or other soy sauce +
   more for serving
   A few drops sesame oil, optional
   Salt and pepper**

- ½ **pound wonton skins**
- 6 **tablespoons peanut oil**
- ½ **teaspoon minced fresh ginger**
- 1 **tablespoon sesame seeds
   Salt and pepper**

METHOD

PREPARATION: *For the filling,* cut the scallions into thin slices. In a meat grinder or food processor, grind the meat to a coarse texture, being careful not to overprocess. Stir in ¼ of the scallions, 2 teaspoons tamari, the sesame oil, ¼ teaspoon salt, and ⅛ teaspoon pepper.

Bring a large pot of salted water to a boil. Put about 1 tablespoon of the filling in the center of a wonton skin. Brush the edges of the skin with warm water, top with another skin, and press gently around the filling to seal edges. Repeat until all the filling is used. Slide wontons into boiling water, stirring gently, and cook for 2 minutes. Drain carefully and plunge into cold water to stop cooking. Drain again. Toss with 1 tablespoon of the peanut oil.

Mince the ginger. In a large frying pan, heat 1 tablespoon peanut oil over medium heat. Add the sesame seeds and cook, stirring frequently, until just golden, about 1 minute. Stir in the ginger. Add the remaining scallions and cook until soft, about 2 minutes. Season to taste with salt and pepper.

Recipe can be made up to this point several hours ahead.

COOKING AND SERVING: Heat 2 more tablespoons of the peanut oil over medium heat. Brown the wontons in batches, adding remaining 2 tablespoons peanut oil between additions, or use 2 pans. Cook until both sides are golden, about 4 minutes total. Top wontons with the scallion-sesame mixture. Serve additional tamari on the side for dipping.

YIELD: 4 servings

WHERE TO FIND WONTON SKINS

Wonton skins, which are thinner than egg roll wrappers, are made daily in cities with a Chinese community and can be bought in Asian markets in packages of 100 for around a dollar. However, if you are nowhere near an Asian market, don't despair— more and more supermarkets are carrying them in the produce section.

Pamela Parseghian
Food editor
COOK'S Magazine

Artichokes and Shrimp with Green Goddess Dressing

VINCENT LEE

Green Goddess dressing, a 1950s favorite, is as elegant as the artichokes and shrimp it's served with when it's made with fresh herbs and homemade mayonnaise.

INGREDIENTS

Green Goddess Dressing

- 2 cups mayonnaise (page 54)
- 1 small clove garlic
- 2 scallions
- 4 anchovies
- 6 tablespoons chopped parsley
- 1 tablespoon chopped tarragon
- ¼ cup chopped chives
  Cayenne pepper
- 2 tablespoons lemon juice or tarragon vinegar
  Salt and pepper

- ¼ small onion
- 1 lemon
- 4 artichokes
- ¼ cup coarse salt, approximately
- 20 shrimp, in the shell (about ¾ pound total)
- ¼ cup parsley stems

METHOD

PREPARATION: *For the Green Goddess Dressing,* make the mayonnaise. Chop the garlic. Mince the scallions. Chop the anchovies, parsley, tarragon, and chives. Put the mayonnaise in a blender or food processor with the garlic, scallions, anchovies, parsley, tarragon, and chives and process until just smooth. Transfer mixture to a large bowl. Season to taste with cayenne, lemon juice, and salt and pepper. Refrigerate until ready to use.

Slice the onion. Halve the lemon. Squeeze juice from ½ the lemon into a bowl of water. Trim ar-

tichoke stems so artichokes will stand up straight and remove any small or damaged leaves from around the base. Cut about an inch off the tops of the artichokes. Trim the sharp points from the leaves with scissors. Put each trimmed artichoke into the bowl of acidulated water to prevent discoloring.

In a covered nonreactive pot, steam the artichokes on a rack until tender, about 30 minutes. To test, pull out an inner leaf and pierce the base of the artichoke with a knife. The leaf should come out easily, and the knife should enter without force. Drain artichokes upside down and cool. Remove innermost leaves and scrape the fuzzy chokes from the center with a small spoon and discard.

Meanwhile, dissolve the salt in a large pot of ice-cold water. Soak shrimp in salted water for 10 minutes. Rinse thoroughly. Cut the remaining ½ lemon into slices and put in a large pot with a couple inches of water. Add the onion and parsley stems and simmer 10 minutes. Add the shrimp and cook until just pink, about 2 minutes, being careful not to overcook. Drain, cool, peel, and devein the shrimp. Squeeze a little lemon juice over them, if desired.

Recipe can be made up to a day ahead.

SERVING: Bring shrimp and artichokes to room temperature if chilled. Put 1 or 2 spoonfuls of dressing into the cavity of each artichoke and arrange shrimp over the leaves. Pass remaining dressing.

YIELD: 4 servings

Moira Hodgson
Free-lance writer
New York, NY

SOUPS

Chilled Avocado Soup

Leek and Onion Soup

Onion Soup with Mushroom Ravioli

Potato Soup with Kale and Bacon

Creamy Mussel and Garlic Soup

Oyster and Spinach Bisque

Chilled Sorrel Soup

Lobster and Corn Consommé

Chicken Soup with Escarole and Tiny Pasta

Turkey and Barley Soup

Chicken Stock

Chilled Avocado Soup

NANCY McFARLAND

The smooth, rich taste and cool color of avocados combine with the spice of jalapeno and bright flavor and color of ripe tomatoes for a glorious study in contrast.

INGREDIENTS

Avocado Soup

2　small avocados
1　lemon
1　lime
2　cups chicken stock (page 30)
1⅓　cups light cream
　　Salt and pepper

Coriander Salsa

2　small tomatoes
1　2-inch piece cucumber
½　red bell pepper
1　jalapeno pepper
2　scallions
1　small clove garlic
1　tablespoon minced fresh coriander
　　Pinch cumin
　　Salt

METHOD

PREPARATION: *For the Avocado Soup,* pit and peel the avocados. Squeeze 4 teaspoons juice from the lemon and 4 teaspoons juice from the lime. Puree the avocados and lemon and lime juices in food processor or food mill. Add the stock, cream, and salt and pepper to taste. Blend well. Chill at least 20 minutes.

For the Coriander Salsa, peel, seed, and chop the tomatoes and cucumber. Seed and chop bell pepper. Seed the jalapeno and mince the flesh. Mince the scallions, garlic, and coriander. Combine all salsa ingredients, or whir garlic and jalapeno in food processor, add remaining ingredients, and process just to combine. Let stand at least 15 minutes at room temperature.

Recipe can be made a few hours ahead.

SERVING: Serve soup with a spoonful of salsa in the center of each bowl.

YIELD: 4 servings

Melanie Barnard
Free-lance writer
New Canaan, CT

Leek and Onion Soup

Tomato, bacon, and yellow pepper lend this earthy onion soup distinctive flavor and color.

INGREDIENTS

2	**leeks**
1	**onion**
1	**small tomato**
1	**small yellow bell pepper**
½	**pound bacon**
	Salt and pepper
1½	**teaspoons fresh thyme or ½ teaspoon dried thyme**
3	**cups chicken stock (page 30)**

METHOD

PREPARATION: Trim the leeks, leaving a couple of inches of green, quarter lengthwise down to the root end, and wash well. Cut into approximately ½-inch pieces. Dice the onion. Peel, seed, and dice the tomato. Char the bell pepper over a gas flame, under the broiler, or on the grill until skin is black-ened and blistered. Peel, core, seed, and cut into thin strips.

Cook the bacon in a large pot until crisp. Remove bacon and chop. Pour off all but 3 tablespoons of fat.

Heat the 3 tablespoons bacon fat over medium-low heat. Add the leeks and ½ teaspoon salt and cook for 3 minutes. Add onion and cook, stirring frequently, until soft, about 10 more minutes. Stir in thyme. Add the stock, season to taste with salt and pepper, and simmer for 5 minutes.

Recipe can be made to this point a few hours ahead.

SERVING: Add the bell pepper and tomato to the soup and cook over low heat until just heated through. Season to taste with salt and pepper. Pass the bacon separately.

YIELD: 4 servings

CLEANING LEEKS

Leeks are very gritty and therefore require extra care to clean. Cut off the root and quarter leek lengthwise cutting down to, but not through, the root end. Rinse under running water, fanning the layers so that all surfaces are exposed to the water.

Pamela Parseghian
Food editor
COOK'S Magazine

Onion Soup with Mushroom Ravioli

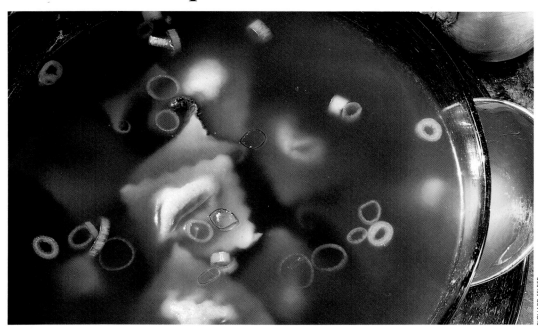

So sophisticated, yet so soothing.

For the Mushroom Ravioli, *put a strip of dough over the filling and press down firmly between each mound.*

INGREDIENTS

½ recipe Egg Pasta (page 66)

Mushroom Stuffing
¼ pound mushrooms
¼ cup white wine
1 shallot
1 tablespoon butter
Salt and pepper
¼ cup heavy cream

Onion Stock
4 onions
2 tablespoons butter
Salt and pepper
½ teaspoon dried thyme
7 cups chicken stock (page 30)
2 tablespoons tamari or other soy sauce

Oil for tossing
2 ounces fresh wild mushrooms, such as chanterelles (about 6 mushrooms)
1 scallion top
1 tablespoon butter
Salt and pepper

METHOD

PREPARATION: Make the Egg Pasta.

For the stuffing, whir the mushrooms, wine, and shallot together in a food processor, or mince the mushrooms and shallot by hand and stir into wine. Melt the butter in a frying pan, add the mushroom mixture, and season to taste with salt and pepper. Cook over medium heat, stirring frequently, until the liquid is reduced and the mixture begins to stick to the bottom of the pan, about 15 minutes. Stir in the cream, season with salt and pepper, and simmer until very thick, about 15 minutes more. Watch closely, stirring frequently toward the end of cooking time to avoid scorching. Chill.

For the stock, cut the onions into thin slices. Melt the butter in a large pot, add the onions, and season with about ½ teaspoon salt. Cook over medium-low heat, stirring frequently, until caramelized but not scorched, about 30 minutes. Stir in thyme. Add chicken stock, bring to a simmer, and cook for 45 minutes. Season to taste with soy sauce and salt and pepper. Strain and discard the onions.

Recipe can be made to this point several days ahead.

Divide the Egg Pasta dough into 4 portions and roll out as thin as possible by hand or with a pasta machine. Brush one strip lightly with water. Mound filling by ¼ teaspoons on top of pasta, spacing mounds about ½ inch apart. Put a second strip of dough on top and press down firmly in between each mound. Cut between each mound with a fluted ravioli cutter-crimper or knife. Repeat with remaining strips.

Cook ravioli in a large pot of boiling, salted water until tender, about 2 minutes. Drain, rinse with cold water, and toss gently with a little oil to prevent sticking.

Recipe can be made to this point a day ahead.

Trim wild mushrooms and cut into thin slices. Cut the scallion top into very thin slices on an angle.

Recipe can be made to this point a couple of hours ahead.

COOKING AND SERVING: Add the ravioli to the onion stock, bring to a simmer, and heat through. Melt the tablespoon of butter in a frying pan, add the sliced mushrooms, and season with salt and pepper. Sauté until just softened, about 2 minutes. Add the mushrooms and sliced scallion top to the soup. Serve at once.

YIELD: 4 servings

Pamela Parseghian
Food editor
COOK'S Magazine

RICHARD FELBER

Potato Soup with Kale and Bacon

Warm German potato salad inspired this hearty, homestyle soup.

INGREDIENTS

2	pounds boiling potatoes
¾	pound bacon
1	bunch kale (about 1 pound)
1	clove garlic
	Salt and pepper
1	cup heavy cream
1	bunch chives, optional
5	teaspoons balsamic vinegar

METHOD

PREPARATION: Peel potatoes and put in a pot with enough cold, salted water to cover. Cover and bring to a boil. Lower heat, uncover, and simmer until done, about 25 minutes. Drain, reserving the cooking liquid. Break up the potatoes with a potato masher; they should be lumpy, not smooth.

Cook the bacon until crisp. Drain and chop. Pour off all but 2 tablespoons of the bacon fat, reserving the extra fat.

Stem and chop the kale. Mince the garlic. Cook half the kale and half the garlic in the 2 tablespoons bacon fat over medium heat until kale is wilted, about 1 minute. Season with salt and pepper and transfer to a bowl. Repeat with remaining garlic and kale. Use reserved bacon fat as needed. Return all the kale to the frying pan and add the heavy cream. Simmer over low heat until the kale is tender, about 10 minutes. Mince the chives.

Recipe can be made to this point several hours ahead.

COOKING AND SERVING: Combine potatoes with about 4 cups of the reserved cooking liquid in a large pot. Add more cooking liquid or water if too thick. Add kale mixture to the pot and bring to a simmer. Season to taste with vinegar and salt and pepper.

Pour into bowls and sprinkle with chives and bacon.

YIELD: 4 servings

Pamela Parseghian
Food editor
COOK'S Magazine

Creamy Mussel and Garlic Soup

Soup needn't be an all-day project; this rich, heady, warming soup can be made in under an hour.

INGREDIENTS

- 5 cloves garlic
- 3 pounds mussels (about 3½ dozen)
- ¾ cup water
- ¾ cup white wine
- 1 red bell pepper
- 3 tablespoons butter
- ¼ pound spiral-shaped dry pasta, such as rotini
  Oil for tossing
- 2 cups heavy cream
  Salt and coarse black pepper
  Cayenne, optional

METHOD

PREPARATION: Peel the garlic. Scrub and debeard the mussels. In a large pot, combine the garlic, water, wine, and mussels. Cover and bring to a boil, stirring mussels occasionally. Cook until shells just open, about 1 minute. Strain mussels and reserve liquid and garlic. Remove mussels from their shells, working over a bowl to catch juices. Strain cooking liquid and juices through a sieve lined with cheesecloth or a coffee filter. Bring to a boil and reduce by half, about 5 minutes.

Mince the cooked garlic. Cut the bell pepper into thin, 1½-inch-long strips. Melt the butter in a large pot, add the garlic, and cook for a few seconds. Add the bell pepper strips and cook until just wilted, about 2 minutes. Add the reduced mussel liquid.

Cook pasta in boiling, salted water until tender. Drain, rinse under cold water, and drain again. Toss with a little oil.

Recipe can be completed to this point several hours ahead.

SERVING: Reheat the soup, if necessary. Whisk in the cream and season to taste with salt and coarse black pepper and a pinch of cayenne pepper. Add the cooked pasta and mussels, heat just until warm, and serve.

YIELD: 4 servings

Pamela Parseghian
Food editor
COOK'S Magazine

Oyster and Spinach Bisque

Oysters and spinach team up in this special soup, an innovative rendition of the classic Oysters Rockefeller.

SHUCKING OYSTERS

You can protect your hand from potential disaster by holding the oyster in a folded dishcloth or in a pot holder. To open oyster, insert a sturdy knife next to the hinge. Twist the knife to open the oyster. Run knife along the top shell to dislodge the muscle and, finally, cut the oyster out from the bottom shell.

INGREDIENTS

2	pounds fresh oysters (about 2 dozen)
1	small onion
½	rib celery
1	leek
1½	cloves garlic
¾	pound spinach
4	tablespoons butter
2	tablespoons flour
⅓	cup white wine
2⅔	cups heavy cream
	Salt and pepper
	Cayenne pepper
	Grated nutmeg

METHOD

PREPARATION: Shuck the oysters over a bowl to catch liquor. Strain oyster liquor through a sieve lined with several layers of cheesecloth or a coffee filter and reserve. Mince the onion, celery, leek, and garlic.

Put the spinach in a pot of boiling, salted water to cover, return to a boil, and drain immediately. Press down on the spinach to remove any excess water.

In a large pot, melt the butter and sauté the onion, celery, leek, and garlic over medium-low heat until soft, about 10 minutes. Add the flour and continue cooking, stirring, for 3 minutes. Gradually add the wine and reserved oyster liquor. Bring to a boil. Add the spinach, stirring frequently to prevent scorching. Add the oysters and continue to cook over medium heat only until the edges of the oysters curl, 3 to 5 minutes.

Transfer the mixture to a food processor and chop, being careful not to overprocess—the consistency should not be entirely smooth.

Return to pan, add 2⅓ cups of the cream, and heat gently. Season to taste with salt and black pepper and cayenne pepper.

Recipe can be made several hours ahead. Whip the remaining ⅓ cup cream lightly. This can be done an hour ahead.

SERVING: Reheat soup if necessary and pour into bowls. Spoon dollops of whipped cream on top and dust with a grating of nutmeg.

YIELD: 4 servings

Lydia Shire
Executive Chef
Four Seasons Hotel
Los Angeles, CA

Chilled Sorrel Soup

Sorrel is the perfect tart complement to an array of fish and shellfish in this summertime soup.

INGREDIENTS

- 1 shallot
- 1 teaspoon chopped fresh thyme *or* ¼ teaspoon dried thyme
- 1 clove garlic
  Salt and pepper
- ¼ pound sorrel
- 2 carrots
- 3 ribs celery
- 1 leek
- ½ cup shredded savoy cabbage
- ⅓ pound swordfish steak *or* ¼ pound fillet
- ⅓ pound salmon steak *or* ¼ pound fillet
- ⅓ pound large shrimp, in the shell
- 2 small boiling potatoes
- 1½ teaspoons olive oil
- ½ cup dry white wine
- 5 cups cold water
- ⅓ pound bay scallops
- 2 ripe avocados
- 1 teaspoon lemon juice
- ¼ cup sour cream

METHOD

PREPARATION: Mince the shallot. Chop the fresh thyme. Mash the garlic with a pinch of salt. Reserve a few small leaves of the sorrel for garnish and clean and remove stems from about three quarters of the rest; cut the leaves crosswise into strips. Cut the carrots into thin slices. Dice the celery. Quarter the leek lengthwise down to the root end, rinse under cold water, and then cut into thin slices. Slice the cabbage into thin shreds. Skin and bone the swordfish and salmon, cut in half lengthwise, and then into ½-inch dice. Peel shrimp, cut in half lengthwise, and devein. Peel the potatoes and cut them into small dice.

In a large saucepan, heat the olive oil. Add the shallot and sauté over medium-high heat until soft, about 1 minute. Add the thyme and garlic and sauté until garlic is soft, about 3 minutes. Stir in the cut sorrel and the carrots, celery, leek, cabbage, and potatoes. Add the wine, water, and salt and pepper to taste. Cover and bring just to a boil. Lower the heat and simmer until all the ingredients are tender, about 8 minutes.

Remove from heat and stir in the swordfish, salmon, shrimp, and scallops. Cool to room temperature and then cover and chill in the refrigerator.

Recipe can be made to this point several hours ahead.

SERVING: Remove the stems from the remaining quarter of the sorrel and cut the leaves crosswise into thin strips. Peel the avocados, coat them with the lemon juice, and push through a sieve. Stir the sorrel, avocado, and sour cream into the chilled soup. Adjust the seasoning with salt and pepper. Put in bowls and garnish with the whole reserved sorrel leaves.

YIELD: 4 servings

Pamela Parseghian
Food editor
COOK'S Magazine

Lobster and Corn Consommé

This black-tie soup can be prepared almost completely the day before serving.

INGREDIENTS

- 2 **lobsters (about 1½ pounds each)**
- 2 **quarts + 1 cup water**
- 3 **tomatoes**
- 2 **scallions**
- 1 **rib celery**
- ½ **cup parsley stems**
- 8 **cloves garlic**
- 1 **small onion**
- ½ **teaspoon dried thyme**
- 1 **bay leaf**
- 2 **cups white wine**
- **Salt and coarse black pepper**
- 3 **egg whites**
- 1 **ear corn *or* ½ cup frozen corn kernels**
- **Parsley for garnish**

METHOD

PREPARATION: Put lobsters in a pot with 1 cup of water, cover, and steam about 7 minutes. Remove lobsters, strain, and reserve the lobster cooking liquid. When lobsters are cool, remove the meat, reserving shells. Halve thorax lengthwise with a large chef's knife and remove the gelatinous sac behind the eyes. Quarter the thorax widthwise.

Core and quarter tomatoes. Chop the scallion bulbs. Slice the scallion tops on an angle into very thin strips and reserve separately. Chop the celery, parsley stems, garlic, and onion.

In a large pot, combine the lobster shells, tomatoes, scallion bulbs, celery, parsley stems, garlic, onion, thyme, bay leaf, white wine, remaining 2 quarts of water, and reserved strained lobster cooking liquid. Season to taste with salt and pepper. Bring to a boil, lower heat, and simmer for 2 hours, skimming as needed. Strain and chill.

Whisk the egg whites and add to the chilled stock. Slowly bring stock to a simmer over low heat, stirring until egg whites coagulate and begin to rise to the surface. Gently push egg whites from center, leaving a hole large enough for a ladle to fit through. Cook for 30 minutes. Gently strain the stock by ladling it through a sieve lined with several layers of cheesecloth or a coffee filter. Strain again if not absolutely clear. Season to taste with salt.

Cook the ear of corn in boiling, salted water until tender, about 4 minutes. Cut kernels from the ear and reserve.

Recipe can be made to this point a day ahead.

SERVING: Scrape away any white substance the lobster has given off, so that it won't cloud the consommé. Cut the lobster meat into bite-size pieces, leaving the claws whole if desired.

Reheat consommé. Add the corn, a sprinkling of pepper, and lobster meat and heat through. Sprinkle with reserved sliced scallion tops and parsley leaves.

YIELD: 4 servings

SHELLING A LOBSTER

To remove lobster meat, twist off the claws and the tail. Remove the tail meat by laying the tail on its side and pressing down firmly so that the shell cracks. Then, grasp the tail bottom-side up with your thumbs along each side, and pull sides away until meat emerges. To remove the claw meat in one piece, rock the pincer shell back and forth and pull off. Crack the claws with the dull side of a chef's knife and slide the meat out.

For the Lobster and Corn Consommé, remove the gelatinous sac from the lobster's head.

Pamela Parseghian
Food editor
COOK'S Magazine

Chicken Soup with Escarole and Tiny Pasta

NANCY McFARLAND

Chicken soup, guaranteed to comfort, gets a lift from shredded escarole, fresh parsley, and grated Parmesan cheese.

INGREDIENTS

1 **3-pound chicken**
1 **bouquet garni of parsley, bay leaf, and thyme**
3 **cups water**
3 **cups chicken stock (page 30)**
1 **small head escarole (about ½ pound)**
2 **leeks *or* 1 onion**
2 **carrots**
2 **tablespoons minced parsley**
1 **ounce Parmesan cheese (about ¼ cup grated)**
2 **ounces small, dry pasta, such as tubettini, pastina, or orzo (about ¼ cup)**
Salt and pepper

METHOD

PREPARATION: Cut up the chicken. Put the parts (including back and giblets, but not liver), bouquet garni, water, and stock in a large, heavy pot and bring to a boil. Lower heat and simmer, covered, until the chicken is cooked through, about 15 minutes.

Remove chicken, reserving stock and discarding the giblets, back, and bouquet garni. When chicken is cool enough to handle, remove meat from the bones and cut into bite-size pieces.

Recipe can be prepared to this point a day ahead.

Wash and trim the escarole. Cut escarole into thin slices across the leaf. Wash the leeks by quartering lengthwise down to the root end and rinsing under cold water. Cut leeks and carrots into thin slices. Mince the parsley. Grate the cheese.

Recipe can be made to this point several hours ahead.

COOKING AND SERVING: Return stock to a boil, add the pasta, carrots, and leeks, and cook until pasta is tender. Add the escarole to the soup, return to a simmer, and add the chicken and parsley. Season to taste with salt and pepper.

Pour soup into large bowls and sprinkle with grated cheese.

YIELD: 4 servings

Melanie Barnard
Free-lance writer
New Canaan, CT

Turkey and Barley Soup

Hearty, wholesome, but certainly not boring, turkey and barley make this soup comforting. Snow peas give it crunch and color.

TIME SAVER

While homemade turkey stock makes this soup especially delicious, you can shorten cooking time and use up leftover turkey by substituting 1½ quarts chicken stock for the turkey stock and already cooked turkey for the fresh breast.

INGREDIENTS

Turkey Stock

4	pounds turkey wings and/or drumsticks
	Salt and pepper
3	ribs celery
2	carrots
2	onions
2	cloves garlic
10 to 15	parsley stems
½	teaspoon dried thyme
6	whole peppercorns
1	bay leaf
½	cup dry white wine
2½	quarts water, approximately

⅔	cup pearl barley
1	pound boneless turkey breast
1	cup snow peas
2	tablespoons butter
	Salt and pepper

METHOD

PREPARATION: *For the Turkey Stock*, heat oven to 400°F. Chop the turkey wings or drumsticks into small pieces. Put the turkey into a roasting pan, sprinkle lightly with salt and pepper, and roast, stirring occasionally, until golden, about 40 minutes.

Chop the celery, carrots, onions, and garlic. Add the chopped vegetables, parsley stems, thyme, peppercorns, and bay leaf to the roasting pan and cook in oven for about 5 minutes more. Transfer mixture to a large stockpot. Add the wine to the roasting pan and scrape with a wooden spoon over high heat to deglaze. Pour into the pot along with enough cold water to cover well, about 2½ quarts. Bring just to a boil, skim, lower heat, and simmer for about 3 hours, skimming as necessary. Strain and season with salt and pepper to taste. You should have about 1½ quarts.

Stock can be made a week ahead.

Cover the barley with salted water and cook until tender, about 1 hour. Drain.

Barley can be cooked several days ahead.

Cut the turkey breast into bite-size pieces. Remove strings from the snow peas and cut the snow peas on an angle into ⅛-inch-wide strips.

Recipe can be made to this point several hours ahead.

COOKING AND SERVING: Heat the stock. In a large frying pan, melt the butter and add the turkey. Season with salt and pepper to taste. Sauté over high heat until just cooked through, about 3 minutes. Add the snow peas and stir to combine. Add the barley, turkey, and snow peas to the stock and adjust the seasonings. Return to a simmer. Pour into bowls.

YIELD: 4 servings

Pamela Parseghian
Food editor
COOK'S Magazine

RICHARD FELBER

Chicken Stock

FREEZING CHICKEN STOCK

With chicken stock in the freezer, making homemade soup is a breeze. Save stray chicken parts and bones in the freezer until you have enough for a batch of stock. There's no need to defrost the chicken before you simmer with vegetables. When stock is finished, pour into small containers so that you don't have to defrost more than you need.

INGREDIENTS

1   large onion
3   cloves
4   cloves garlic
2   ribs celery
2   carrots
4   pounds chicken bones and parts, such as carcasses, wing tips, necks, and gizzards (no liver)
1   bay leaf
4   whole peppercorns
    Salt
½   teaspoon dried thyme
6   sprigs parsley

METHOD

PREPARATION: Halve the onion and stick the cloves into it. Peel the garlic. Chop the celery and carrots.

Put all ingredients except thyme and parsley into a large stock pot and add cold water to cover bones and vegetables completely. Salt very lightly. Bring water to a boil, skimming any foam that rises to the top. Add thyme and parsley. Simmer, partially covered, about 3 hours. Strain stock, reduce to about 2 quarts, cool, and chill.

Keep in the refrigerator for up to a week or freeze.

YIELD: about 2 quarts

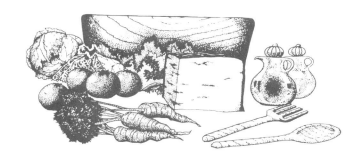

SALADS

Smoked Duck Salad

Grilled Scallion and Potato Salad

Bulgur Garden Salad

Seafood and Barley Salad

Grilled-Fish Salad with Oregano Dressing

Squab and Arugula Salad

Fried-Chicken Salad with Sweet Onions

Pork and Shallot Salad

Salami and Cheese Salad

Smoked Duck Salad

Smoky duck and red and yellow peppers combine beautifully with earthy lentil salad in this ideal fall dish.

INGREDIENTS

    2   whole boneless duck breasts, split
        Salt and pepper
    2   cups lentils
    2   small cloves garlic
    2   scallions
    2   red bell peppers
    2   yellow bell peppers
    4   cups chicken stock (page 30)
    1   tablespoon balsamic vinegar
    ¾   cup olive oil
    3   tablespoons lemon juice
        Arugula or watercress sprigs for
        garnish
        Black olives for garnish

METHOD

PREPARATION: Season duck breasts with salt and pepper and smoke in water smoker or over an indirect fire in a kettle grill until it tests done and is pink inside, 30 to 40 minutes if using water smoker, 15 to 20 minutes if using kettle grill.

Rinse and pick over lentils. Mince the garlic. Cut the scallions on an angle into thin slices. Roast red and yellow bell peppers over a gas flame, under the broiler, or on the grill until the skin is blistered. Peel the peppers and cut into 1-inch strips.

In a saucepan, bring the lentils and stock to a boil, covered. Lower heat and simmer until lentils are just tender but not mushy and liquid has been absorbed, about 30 minutes. Cool.

In a bowl, toss bell peppers with balsamic vinegar and garlic. Season to taste with salt and pepper and set aside. Season lentils to taste with salt and pepper and add the olive oil, lemon juice, and scallions.

Recipe can be made to this point a couple of days ahead.

SERVING: Slice the cooled duck on an angle and arrange on plates. Put marinated pepper strips and lentil salad alongside. Garnish with arugula and olives. Serve at cool room temperature.

YIELD: 4 servings

Richard Sax
Free-lance writer
New York, New York

Grilled Scallion and Potato Salad

VINCENT LEE

This potato salad is equally at home accompanying steak or hamburgers. It is also ideal for picnics since it will keep for hours without refrigeration.

INGREDIENTS

- **1 pound new potatoes**
- **4 scallions**
- **6 tablespoons olive oil**
- **Salt and pepper**
- **2 tablespoons white vinegar**

METHOD

PREPARATION: Heat the grill. Slice unpeeled potatoes into ⅛-inch-thick rounds. Toss potatoes and whole scallions with 2 tablespoons of olive oil, 1 teaspoon salt, and ½ teaspoon pepper. Grill potatoes and scallions, turning once, until they test done and are golden brown, about 8 minutes. Grill in batches if necessary.

Whisk together the remaining 4 tablespoons olive oil and vinegar in a large bowl. Cut the scallions and potatoes into bite-size pieces. Toss potatoes and scallions with the oil and vinegar mixture. Season to taste with salt and pepper.

SERVING: Serve warm or at room temperature. The salad is better if it's never refrigerated. It will keep at room temperature for several hours.

YIELD: 4 servings

Pamela Parseghian
Food editor
COOK'S Magazine

Bulgur Garden Salad

Whole grains have a reputation for being homely as well as wholesome, but bulgur comes alive with colorful vegetables and a distinctive jalapeno and coriander vinaigrette.

BULGUR— THE QUICK GRAIN

Grains are the seeds from grasses and food plants. They are a staple throughout the world because they are hardy, growing in poor soil and harsh climates, and they are astonishingly nutritious. Bulgur, also known as cracked wheat, is a partially processed grain, and so requires a slightly reduced cooking time. For instance, the salad here can be made in less than an hour. Use a medium or coarse bulgur for this salad.

Michael McLaughlin
Chef/owner
The Manhattan Chili Company
New York, NY

INGREDIENTS

2 cups bulgur
Salt
2 red bell peppers
2 tomatoes
3 zucchini
4 scallions

Herb and Pepper Vinaigrette

1 jalapeno pepper
1 cup fresh coriander
1 cup fresh mint
5 tablespoons white-wine vinegar
Salt and pepper
¾ cup olive oil

Salad greens, such as romaine, arugula, watercress, or Bibb, to line plates
½ pound sharp, white, crumbly cheese, such as feta or chèvre

METHOD

PREPARATION: Put bulgur in a bowl. In a small saucepan, bring 3 cups water to a boil and stir in 2½ teaspoons salt. Pour boiling water over the bulgur.

Let stand, stirring once or twice, for 45 minutes. Strain bulgur, pressing with back of a spoon to extract any water that hasn't been absorbed. Return bulgur to bowl.

Char bell peppers over a gas flame, under a broiler, or on a grill until skin is blackened. Cool enough to handle. Peel and seed peppers and cut into ½-inch dice. Peel and seed tomatoes and cut into ½-inch dice. Cut zucchini into ½-inch dice. Slice the scallions. Toss bell peppers, tomatoes, zucchini, and scallions with the bulgur.

For the Herb and Pepper Vinaigrette, stem and seed jalapeno. Blend jalapeno, coriander, mint, vinegar, and ½ teaspoon salt in a food processor until smooth. With machine running, slowly add the oil.

Pour the dressing over bulgur salad and toss to combine. Adjust seasoning with salt and pepper. Wash and dry the greens.

Recipe can be made to this point several hours ahead.

SERVING: Line 4 plates with greens. Mound bulgur salad onto the greens. Crumble cheese over all.

YIELD: 4 servings

Seafood and Barley Salad

This salad makes an ideal summertime meal—cool, refreshing, and satisfying.

INGREDIENTS

1⅓ cups **pearl barley**
¾ pound **bay scallops**
3 ribs **celery**
1 **red onion**
¼ cup **Mediterranean black olives**
¾ pound **shrimp, in the shell**

Lemon and Basil Vinaigrette
1 **lemon**
1½ cups **fresh basil**
  Salt and pepper
⅔ cup **olive oil**

Sprigs of basil for garnish, optional

METHOD

PREPARATION: Bring a large pot of salted water to a boil. Stir in barley, lower heat, and simmer, un- covered, until barley is tender, about 1 hour. Drain.

Barley can be cooked several days ahead.

Trim scallops. Dice the celery and onion. Pit and chop the olives.

Bring a pot of salted water to a boil. Add shrimp. After 1 minute, add the scallops and cook 1 more minute. Drain the seafood and cool to room temperature. Shell the shrimp, slice in half lengthwise, and devein.

Toss seafood with barley. Stir in the celery and onion.

For the Lemon and Basil Vinaigrette, squeeze 2 tablespoons juice from the lemon. Whir basil, lemon juice, and ½ teaspoon salt in a food processor until almost smooth. Scrape down the sides of the bowl. With machine running, slowly add oil.

Pour dressing over the salad and toss well. Season to taste with salt and pepper.

Recipe can be completed several hours ahead.

SERVING: Garnish salad with chopped olives and sprigs of basil if desired. Serve cool or at room temperature.

YIELD: 4 servings

Michael McLaughlin
Chef/owner
The Manhattan Chili Company
New York, NY

Grilled-Fish Salad with Oregano Dressing

RICHARD FELBER

The classic salade niçoise *is updated and dressed up by using an untraditional dressing and seared fresh fish instead of the more typical canned tuna.*

INGREDIENTS

Oregano Dressing

- ½ cup fresh oregano or marjoram leaves
- 2 cloves garlic
- 1 egg
- 3 tablespoons red-wine vinegar
  Salt and pepper
- 1 cup olive oil

- 6 small new potatoes
- 3 eggs
- 1 pound green beans
- 2 tomatoes
- 1½ pounds tuna, salmon, or swordfish steaks
  Salt and pepper
- 2 tablespoons olive oil
- ⅓ cup Mediterranean black olives

METHOD

PREPARATION: *For the Oregano Dressing,* stem oregano to make ½ cup leaves. In a food processor, combine the oregano, garlic, egg, vinegar, 1 teaspoon salt, and ¼ teaspoon pepper and process until smooth, about 1 minute. With the machine running, add the oil in a slow, thin stream. Adjust seasoning to taste and refrigerate.

Put potatoes in a pot with cold, salted water to cover. Cover pot and bring to a boil. Uncover and continue cooking until tender, about 15 minutes. Drain.

Put eggs in a saucepan, cover with water, and bring to a simmer. Cover, remove from heat, let sit at least 12 minutes, and drain. Peel the eggs.

Cook the beans in a pot of boiling, salted water until tender, about 10 minutes. Drain, refresh under cold, running water, and drain again.

Peel and seed the tomatoes and cut flesh into small dice.

Recipe can be completed to this point several hours ahead.

Pat the fish dry and season with salt and pepper. In a heavy frying pan, heat the oil until very hot. Add the fish and cook over high heat, turning once, until well seared but still moist inside, about 3 minutes total. Remove and cool to room temperature.

Recipe can be made to this point about 1 hour ahead.

SERVING: Bring dressing back to room temperature if refrigerated. Slice the potatoes. Quarter the eggs. Flake fish or cut into thin slices and arrange on plates along with the beans, potatoes, eggs, and diced tomatoes. Drizzle each salad with dressing and scatter olives over all. Season with salt and pepper. Pass remaining dressing.

YIELD: 4 servings

Michael McLaughlin
Chef/owner
The Manhattan Chili Company
New York, NY

Squab and Arugula Salad

RICHARD FELBER

This spectacular salad, little more than a grilled bird atop a bed of greens, is a powerful argument that the simplest food can be the most elegant.

WHAT'S IN A NAME?

Squab is actually fledgling pigeon. Unlike its full-grown counterpart, however, which has tough, gamy meat, the meat of a 4-week-old squab is tender, sweet, and moist. Squabs range from ¾ to 1¼ pounds, so plan on one bird per person.

INGREDIENTS

    4   **squabs (about 1 pound each)**
    3   **bunches arugula (about 10 ounces)**
    1   **pint cherry or small yellow tomatoes**

Black-Olive Vinaigrette
  ½ **cup chopped Mediterranean black olives**
  ⅓ **cup sherry vinegar**
      Salt and pepper
1¼ **cups olive oil + more for rubbing squabs**

METHOD

PREPARATION: Cut along one side of the backbone of each squab. Spread the bird open and cut off the backbone by cutting along its other side. Cut off the wing tips. Pat squabs dry.

   Stem, wash, and dry the arugula. Halve the tomatoes.

For the Black-Olive Vinaigrette, pit and chop the olives. In a small bowl, combine the vinegar and salt and pepper to taste. Whisk in the oil and add the olives.

   Recipe can be made to this point several hours ahead.

COOKING AND SERVING: Heat the grill. If desired, soak a handful of wood chips, such as cherry or apple, in water for 20 minutes. Rub squabs with oil, throw the chips on the fire, and grill the birds, turning once, until crisp and dark brown on the outside, still slightly pink and juicy on the inside, about 20 minutes total, or preheat oven to 350°F and roast for about 45 minutes.

   Put arugula on plates. Scatter tomato halves over arugula and center 1 squab on top of each serving. Whisk the vinaigrette and pour over salad. Serve warm.

YIELD: 4 servings

Michael McLaughlin
Chef/owner
The Manhattan Chili Company
New York, NY

Fried-Chicken Salad with Sweet Onions

BUYING ONIONS

While onions can last for months, their quality deteriorates in winter. Look for firm, dry onions; moisture at the top may indicate mildew. Never buy onions that are sprouting. This means they are old and probably overly pungent.

Onions are at their best from the springtime on throughout the summer when they are sweeter and a greater variety is available. This salad becomes a true Southern specialty with the addition of Vidalia onions from Georgia. Walla Wallas from Washington State, Hawaiian Mauis, and Texan Y-33s are also excellent. (Onions from Texas and Hawaii are available as early as late winter.)

Anne Byrn
Food editor and restaurant critic
The Atlanta Journal and
The Atlanta Constitution

The best of old and new combine as southern fried chicken gets freshened up in a thoroughly modern salad.

VINCENT LEE

INGREDIENTS

- 2 heads Boston or Bibb lettuce
- 8 cherry tomatoes
- 2 ounces mushrooms
- 1 shallot
- 1 tablespoon chopped tarragon *or* 1 teaspoon dried tarragon
- 1 sweet onion, such as Vidalia
- 1 tablespoon capers, optional
- 2 whole chicken breasts (about 3½ pounds total)
- ½ cup flour
  Salt and coarse black pepper
- ½ cup peanut oil
- ⅓ cup milk
- 2 tablespoons white-wine vinegar
- 2 teaspoons Dijon mustard
  Tarragon sprigs for garnish

METHOD

PREPARATION: Wash and dry the lettuce. Halve the tomatoes. Slice the mushrooms. Mince the shallot. Chop the tarragon leaves. Cut the onion into thin slices. Drain the capers. Halve and bone the chicken breasts and cut into ½-inch-wide strips. In a shallow bowl, mix flour with ½ teaspoon salt and ¼ teaspoon coarse black pepper.

Recipe can be made to this point several hours ahead.

COOKING AND SERVING: Heat the oil in a frying pan over medium-high heat. Put the milk in a shallow bowl. Dip chicken strips into milk, then into flour mixture to coat, and fry in the oil, turning once, until golden brown, about 5 minutes total. Drain chicken on paper towels, reserving oil in the pan.

Add vinegar to the oil, stirring with a wooden spoon to deglaze the bottom of the pan. Pour oil and vinegar into a bowl and mix in the mustard. Add mushrooms, the shallot, and chopped tarragon and season to taste with salt and pepper.

Arrange lettuce leaves and tomatoes on 4 salad plates. Put chicken strips on top of lettuce leaves and pour just enough vinaigrette over the salads to moisten leaves. Scatter capers and onion slices on top and garnish with tarragon sprigs. Serve remaining dressing on the side.

YIELD: 4 servings

Pork and Shallot Salad

Sliced tomatoes and hard-cooked eggs make good garnishes for this salad. Accompany it with a chewy bread, and you have a complete meal.

INGREDIENTS

- **4 pork chops (about 2½ pounds total)**
  Salt and pepper
- **6 tablespoons oil**
- **4 large shallots**
- **⅓ cup minced parsley**
- **2 tablespoons red-wine vinegar**

METHOD

PREPARATION: Season pork with salt and pepper. Heat 2 tablespoons of oil in a large frying pan over high heat until very hot. Add pork chops to the pan and cook, turning once, until just done, about 10 minutes total, depending on thickness. Remove the pork chops from the pan and save the pan juices.

Cut the shallots into thin slices. Mince the parsley. Add half of the shallots to the frying pan and cook over medium heat until soft, about 5 minutes. Add the vinegar, stirring with a wooden spoon to deglaze the bottom of the pan. Put the cooked shallots and pan juices in a large bowl.

Remove the pork from the bones, trim, and cut into bite-size cubes. Add the pork and its juices to the shallots. Toss with remaining oil, sliced raw shallots, and parsley. Season to taste with salt and pepper.

The salad can be completed a day ahead.

SERVING: Serve at room temperature or slightly chilled.

YIELD: 4 servings

Pamela Parseghian
Food editor
COOK'S Magazine

Salami and Cheese Salad

RICHARD FELBER

Here is a virtually indestructible salad, perfect for packing into a picnic. Its greatest virtue, though, aside from requiring no cooking, is the speed with which it goes together.

FOR CRISP SALAD GREENS

If possible, wash salad greens at least an hour before serving. Shake off excess water, wrap in paper towels or a dishcloth, and refrigerate. If you plan on crisping lettuce for several hours, place towel-wrapped lettuce in a plastic bag and refrigerate. This will prevent greens from dehydrating.

INGREDIENTS

Balsamic and Mustard Seed Dressing
⅓ cup balsamic vinegar
1 tablespoon yellow mustard seeds
¾ cup olive oil

4 scallions
2 red bell peppers
1 pound salami or other ready-to-eat
   spiced sausage
¾ pound Gruyère or cheddar cheese
5 ears corn *or* 2½ cups frozen kernels
   Salt and pepper
1 head romaine lettuce

METHOD

PREPARATION: *For the dressing,* stir together the vinegar and mustard seeds in a small bowl. Let stand for about 30 minutes. Whisk in the oil.

Cut the scallions, including green tops, into thin slices. Seed the peppers and cut them into ¼-inch dice. Cut both the salami and cheese into ½-inch cubes.

If using fresh, cook ears of corn in boiling, salted water until tender, about 5 minutes. Cool. Cut the kernels from the cobs. Or cook frozen corn in a small amount of water until tender, about 2 minutes. Drain.

In a bowl, combine the scallions, bell peppers, salami, cheese, and corn and toss with the dressing. Season to taste with salt and pepper. Wash and dry the lettuce.

Recipe can be completed a day ahead.

SERVING: Put lettuce leaves on plates and top with a mound of salad.

YIELD: 4 servings

Michael McLaughlin
Chef/owner
The Manhattan Chili Company
New York, NY

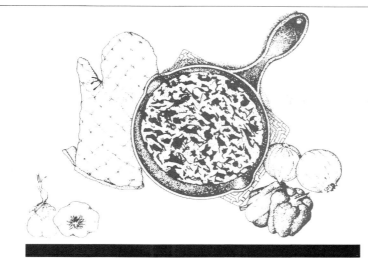

ONE-DISH MAIN COURSES

Caesar Salad with Fried Oysters

In this variation on the classic Caesar Salad, the usual croutons are replaced by crisp fried oysters. With good bread, this salad makes a complete meal.

THE ROOTS OF A FINE SALAD

The original Caesar Salad was created in the 1920s by Caesar Cardini, an Italian immigrant who ran a popular restaurant in Tijuana. The restaurant attracted many Californians, and Caesar Salad gained a big following. Cardini's Italian roots are evident in the dressing's ingredients—garlic, Parmesan cheese, olive oil—as well as in the romaine lettuce, originally brought to the U.S. from the Mediterranean.

For the Caesar Salad, mash the garlic with a pinch of coarse salt using the flat side of a large chef's knife.

Pamela Parseghian
Food editor
COOK'S Magazine

INGREDIENTS

    2   dozen oysters
    ¾   cup flour
        Salt and coarse black pepper
    2   cloves garlic
    2   eggs
    ¼   cup milk
    1½ cups bread crumbs
    1   head romaine lettuce

Caesar Dressing

    1   clove garlic
    2   anchovy fillets *or* 1 teaspoon anchovy
        paste
        Salt and pepper
    3   ounces Parmesan cheese (about ¾
        cup grated)
    2   lemons
    ½   teaspoon white-wine vinegar
    1   egg
    ½   cup olive oil

        Oil for frying

METHOD

PREPARATION: Shuck the oysters and drain. Mix the flour with 1 teaspoon salt and ¼ teaspoon coarse pepper. Using the side of a large knife, mash 2 cloves of garlic with a pinch of salt. In a large bowl, whisk together the garlic paste with the eggs, milk, ½ teaspoon salt and ¼ teaspoon pepper. Put bread crumbs in another large bowl. Dredge the oysters in flour, dip in the egg mixture, and then coat with bread crumbs. Put oysters on a baking sheet in a single layer. Refrigerate until ready to fry.

Wash and dry the lettuce and tear into bite-size pieces.

For the dressing, mash the garlic, the anchovy fillets, and a pinch of salt to a fine paste. Grate the cheese. Squeeze ¼ cup juice from lemons. Whisk together the garlic/anchovy paste, ½ cup of the cheese, the lemon juice, vinegar, and the egg. Whisk in olive oil. Season to taste with salt and pepper.

Recipe can be made to this point several hours ahead.

COOKING AND SERVING: Heat oil for frying to about 350°F. Toss lettuce with dressing. Divide salad among 4 plates. Fry breaded oysters in batches until golden and crisp, about 10 seconds per side. Drain the oysters, sprinkle with salt, and put them on dressed lettuce. Sprinkle with remaining cheese.

YIELD: 4 servings

Pasta with Summer Vegetables and Prosciutto

Pretty and uncomplicated, this dish allows fresh vegetables to shine.

INGREDIENTS

¼	**pound green beans**
1	**small red bell pepper**
1	**zucchini**
1	**yellow squash**
2	**scallions**
1	**teaspoon minced fresh thyme** *or* ½ **teaspoon dried thyme**
½	**pound thin-sliced prosciutto**
½	**pound fusilli or other dry pasta**
3	**tablespoons oil**
1	**tablespoon butter**
	Salt and pepper

METHOD

PREPARATION: Trim the beans and cut into ½-inch pieces. Core, seed, and chop the red bell pepper. Halve the zucchini and yellow squash lengthwise and then slice crosswise. Cut the scallions, including green tops, into thin slices. Mince the thyme. Cut the prosciutto slices into ½-inch pieces.

Recipe can be made to this point a few hours ahead.

COOKING AND SERVING: Cook pasta in a large pot of boiling, salted water. Drain well, return to warm pot, and toss with 1 tablespoon of the oil.

Meanwhile, heat another tablespoon of the oil in a large frying pan. Add ½ tablespoon of the butter and the squash and cook over medium-high heat, tossing frequently, until tender, about 8 minutes. Remove squash from the pan. Add the remaining tablespoon of oil, the remaining ½ tablespoon of butter, and the beans to the frying pan and cook until almost tender, about 3 minutes. Add the red bell pepper and thyme and cook 5 minutes more.

Add squash and bean mixture to the pasta and heat through. Remove from heat. Toss in the prosciutto and scallions and season to taste with salt and pepper.

YIELD: 4 servings

Pamela Parseghian
Food editor
COOK'S Magazine

La Pipérade

This Basque-American specialty is the very essence of Old Country cooking in the Wild West—earthy, simple, and highly flavored.

INGREDIENTS

2 onions
2 cloves garlic
   Salt and pepper
2 large tomatoes
1 green bell pepper
1 red bell pepper
1 small hot red pepper
3 tablespoons olive oil
¼ teaspoon sugar
¼ pound ham
1 tablespoon chopped parsley for garnish
6 eggs

METHOD

PREPARATION: Chop the onions. Using the flat side of a large knife, crush garlic with a pinch of salt. Core, seed, and chop tomatoes. Remove stems, seeds, and ribs from green and red bell peppers and chop. Stem, seed, and mince hot pepper.

In a large frying pan, heat 1½ tablespoons of the olive oil. Add the onions and garlic paste and sauté until onions are wilted, about 5 minutes. Add tomatoes, bell and hot peppers, the sugar, and black pepper to taste. Stir. Cook, covered, over medium heat until vegetables are very soft and mixture has thickened, about 25 minutes. Uncover, increase heat, and reduce mixture for 1 to 2 minutes more.

Recipe can be made to this point several days ahead.

Cut ham into julienne strips. Chop the parsley.

Recipe can be made to this point several hours ahead.

COOKING AND SERVING: In a frying pan, cook ham over low heat in remaining 1½ tablespoons olive oil until browned, about 5 minutes. Remove ham with a slotted spoon and keep warm. Reserve oil in pan.

Beat eggs with a fork and add to vegetables. Heat reserved oil in frying pan and pour in egg mixture. Simmer mixture, stirring, over low heat until eggs just begin to set. Let eggs continue to cook undisturbed until set.

Divide among plates, top with warm ham, and sprinkle with parsley.

YIELD: 4 servings

Elene Margot Kolb
Free-lance writer
New York, NY

Chicken and Avocado Sandwiches

Avocado and Belgian endive make something special out of a chicken sandwich.

INGREDIENTS

Mayonnaise (page 54)
1 tablespoon oil
4 boneless, skinless chicken breasts
(about 1¼ pounds total)
Salt and pepper
1 avocado
1 tablespoon lemon juice
8 slices brioche, challah, French or
Italian bread
1 Belgian endive

METHOD

PREPARATION: Make the mayonnaise.

Heat oil in a frying pan. Sprinkle the chicken with salt and pepper and sear on both sides over medium-high heat, about 5 minutes in all. Add 3 tablespoons water and simmer until cooked through, about 5 minutes more. Remove chicken from the pan and set aside to cool. Cut the chicken breasts in half horizontally.

Recipe can be made to this point several hours ahead.

SERVING: Halve, pit, and skin the avocado and cut into thin slices. Gently toss the avocado with the lemon juice and season with salt and pepper to taste.

Toast bread and spread with mayonnaise. Layer each sandwich with endive leaves, chicken, and avocado.

YIELD: 4 sandwiches

Pamela Parseghian
Food editor
COOK'S Magazine

Spicy Chinese Duck Salad

RICHARD FELBER

All of the components of this salad can be prepared hours ahead, leaving only the assembly for the last minute. For even greater ease, buy a carry-out Peking duck and ask the restaurant to cut it into pieces for you.

To make orange sections, cut off the top and bottom of the orange and then remove the remaining skin in strips including all of the white pith.

Cut the sections of flesh away from the membrane, working over a bowl to catch the juice.

Michael McLaughlin
Chef/owner
The Manhattan Chili Company
New York, NY

INGREDIENTS

Spicy Dressing
1½ teaspoons minced fresh ginger
½ jalapeno or other hot pepper
1 clove garlic
1 egg
1½ teaspoons sugar
1½ tablespoons soy sauce
2 tablespoons red-wine vinegar
1½ teaspoons sesame oil
⅓ cup peanut or vegetable oil
Salt and pepper

1 Peking duck *or* roast duck, recipe follows
1 package dry oriental-style noodles, such as soba or buckwheat (about ½ pound)
3 tablespoons peanut or vegetable oil
2 scallions
2 large oranges

METHOD

PREPARATION: *For the Spicy Dressing,* mince the ginger. Seed the jalapeno. In a food processor, combine the ginger, jalapeno, garlic, egg, sugar, soy sauce, and vinegar and process until smooth, about 1 minute. With the machine running, add the oils in a slow stream. Season to taste with salt and pepper and refrigerate.

Dressing can be completed 2 days ahead.

Roast the duck, if making your own. Cook the noodles in a large pot of boiling, salted water until tender, about 5 minutes. Drain, rinse well under cold water, and drain again. Toss noodles with the 3 tablespoons oil.

Cut the scallions, including green tops, into thin slices. With a sharp knife, peel the oranges, removing all the white pith and cut sections away from the membrane. Remove meat from duck and slice.

Recipe can be completed to this point a couple of hours ahead.

SERVING: Toss ½ the scallions with the noodles, put on plates, and arrange pieces of duck and orange sections on top. Drizzle salads with dressing and sprinkle with remaining scallions.

YIELD: 4 servings

Chinese Roast Duck

INGREDIENTS

1 duck (about 4½ to 5 pounds)
3 tablespoons soy sauce
2 tablespoons molasses
1 tablespoon sesame oil

METHOD

PREPARATION: Trim all loose fat from duck. Prick skin all over. In a small bowl, stir together the soy sauce, molasses, and sesame oil.

Recipe can be made to this point a day ahead.

COOKING: Heat oven to 325°F. Put the duck in a shallow roasting pan and set on a rack in the center of preheated oven. Roast for 2 hours, occasionally removing fat from the pan and pricking the duck skin.

Brush the duck generously with the soy mixture and continue roasting, brushing with the remaining soy mixture every 10 minutes, until the duck is cooked through and is crisp and shiny, about 30 more minutes. Remove the duck from the oven and let cool.

YIELD: 4 servings

Ham and Shrimp Jambalaya Soup

This ham and seafood soup is lighter fare than the traditional creole specialty, but still substantial enough to be the center of a meal.

INGREDIENTS

1	shallot
½	rib celery
1	clove garlic
	Salt and pepper
2	tomatoes *or* 2 canned Italian plum tomatoes
1	tablespoon minced flat-leaf parsley
1	green bell pepper
¼	pound smoked ham
½	pound shrimp, in the shell
1½	teaspoons oil
⅓	cup rice
2	teaspoons tomato paste
2½	cups chicken stock (page 30)
¼	teaspoon cayenne

METHOD

PREPARATION: Heat oven to 350°F. Mince the shallot and celery. Mash the garlic with a pinch of salt. If using fresh tomatoes, peel and seed. Cut tomatoes into ½-inch chunks. Mince the parsley.

Roast the bell pepper over a gas flame, under the broiler, or on a grill until skin is blackened. Peel pepper and cut into ¼-inch strips. Cut the ham into ¼-inch-thick strips. Peel and devein the shrimp.

In a large, ovenproof pan, heat oil over medium-high heat. Add the rice and stir until coated with oil. Stir in shallot and celery. Cook until shallot is just soft, about 2 minutes. Add the mashed garlic, tomatoes, and tomato paste and stir well. Add parsley, bell pepper, chicken stock, black pepper, and cayenne. Bring to a simmer.

Cover and put in preheated oven for 17 minutes. Stir in ham and shrimp and return to oven for 3 minutes.

Recipe can be completed to this point several days ahead.

SERVING: Reheat soup, covered, if necessary, until just heated through, about 5 minutes. Season to taste with salt and pepper and serve.

YIELD: 4 servings

Pamela Parseghian
Food editor
COOK'S Magazine

Cassoulet Soup

This soup, a takeoff on the traditional French cassoulet, is good made a day ahead so flavors meld. Just heat through when ready to serve.

INGREDIENTS

Thyme Croutons

6	slices hearty white bread
1½	teaspoons chopped fresh thyme *or* ½ teaspoon dried thyme
5	tablespoons butter
	Salt

1	pound dried white beans (about 6 cups)
1	tablespoon olive oil
½	pound spicy sausage, such as chorizo
½	pound garlic sausage
1	pig's foot or ½ pound fatback
6	large plum tomatoes or 4 regular tomatoes
1	small onion
2	quarts chicken stock (page 30)
2	carrots
1	rib celery
½	teaspoon dried thyme
1	bay leaf
	Salt and pepper
2	teaspoons chopped parsley

METHOD

PREPARATION: *For the croutons,* trim away the bread crusts and cut bread into small cubes. Chop the thyme. Melt the butter in a large frying pan over medium heat. Add thyme and sprinkle with salt. Add cubed bread and sauté, tossing frequently, until golden brown, about 5 minutes. Drain.

Croutons can be made a few days ahead and stored in an airtight container.

Put beans in a large pot with cold water to cover by 1 inch and soak at least 6 hours. Or bring to a boil, cover, remove from heat, and let sit about 1 hour. Drain and rinse beans.

Heat olive oil over medium-high heat in a large soup pot. Brown sausages and pig's foot until golden, about 10 minutes. Peel, seed, and chop tomatoes. Halve the onion. Add stock, tomatoes, ½ of the onion, 1 carrot, celery, beans, thyme, and bay leaf to the pot and season lightly with salt and pepper. Bring to a simmer over low heat, skimming as needed. Remove sausages from the pot when done, about 10 minutes, and set aside. Continue cooking other ingredients, barely simmering, until beans are tender, about 45 minutes.

Cut remaining carrot and the sausage in half lengthwise and then into thin slices. Dice remaining ½ onion. Remove the cooked celery, carrot, onion, pig's foot, and bay leaf from the pot and discard. Add the sliced raw carrot and cook for 5 minutes. Add diced onion and cook another 5 minutes. Add sausages and heat through.

Recipe can be completed to this point 1 day ahead.

SERVING: Chop the parsley. Reheat soup, if necessary, and pour soup into large bowls. Sprinkle parsley on top. Pass thyme croutons separately.

YIELD: 4 servings

Pamela Parseghian
Food editor
COOK'S Magazine

Pumpkin and Bean Stew

RICHARD FELBER

This hearty stew, developed by James Villas, Food and Wine editor for Town & Country, *is so wholesome and unpretentious that it's revolutionary!*

INGREDIENTS

- 1 cup dried white beans
- 1 large onion
- 1 clove garlic
- ½ small chili pepper
- ½ green bell pepper
- 1 large tomato
- ¼ pound cured country ham
- 1½ pounds pumpkin or hubbard squash
- 1½ tablespoons butter
- ¼ cup olive oil
- 1 cup chicken stock (page 30), + more if necessary
- ¼ teaspoon dried thyme
- ¼ teaspoon dried summer savory
   Salt and pepper

METHOD

PREPARATION: Put beans in a large pot with cold water to cover by 1 inch and soak at least 6 hours. Or bring to a boil, cover, remove from heat, and let sit about 1 hour. Drain and rinse the beans.

Chop the onion. Mince the garlic and the chili pepper. Chop the bell pepper and tomato. Dice the ham. Peel pumpkin and remove the seeds. Cut the flesh into 1-inch chunks.

In a large, heavy pot, heat the butter and oil. Add the onion, garlic, chili pepper, and bell pepper. Sauté over medium heat, stirring occasionally, until soft, about 5 minutes.

Add the beans, tomato, ham, stock, thyme, summer savory, and salt and black pepper to taste. Bring to a boil, lower heat, cover, and simmer until the beans are tender, 1 to 2 hours.

Stir the pumpkin into the pot and add more stock or water if the stew is too thick. Cover and continue to simmer until pumpkin is tender, about 30 minutes more.

Recipe can be completed several days ahead.

SERVING: Reheat the stew over low heat if necessary. Season with salt and pepper to taste and serve.

YIELD: 4 servings

James Villas
Food and Wine editor
Town & Country Magazine

Duck Choucroute

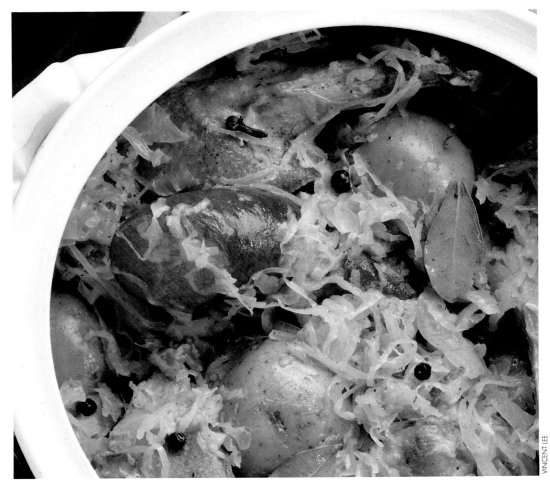

VINCENT LEE

The traditional Alsatian choucroute garnie *is made entirely with pork. The recipe here calls for duck, as well as sausage and smoked bacon, and can also be made with goose or even chicken.*

INGREDIENTS

½	**pound smoked slab bacon**
3	**pounds sauerkraut**
1	**3- to 4-pound duck or goose *or* 2½ pounds chicken thighs**
	Salt and pepper
½	**pound fresh kielbasa or other smoked sausage**
2	**onions**
1	**large clove garlic**
1	**ham hock, optional**
¾	**cup white wine**
1¼	**cups chicken stock (page 30)**
1	**tablespoon juniper berries**
½	**teaspoon peppercorns**
1	**teaspoon dried thyme**
3	**cloves**
1	**bay leaf**
6	**small red potatoes**

METHOD

PREPARATION: Cut bacon into large pieces and cook in a large, deep pot over low heat, stirring occasionally, until fat is rendered, about 20 minutes. Remove bacon with a slotted spoon and set aside. Reserve the bacon fat in pot.

Drain sauerkraut. If using duck or goose, cut into 8 pieces. Season lightly with salt. Cut sausage into 4 pieces. Slice onions and garlic. In the bacon fat, sear poultry, sausage, and ham hock over medium-high heat until golden, about 10 minutes. Cook in batches if necessary. Remove meats from the pot. Save ⅓ cup of the fat and all browned bits in the pot; pour out any excess fat.

Lower heat to medium. Add sliced onions and garlic to pot. Cook until soft, stirring with a wooden spoon, about 5 minutes. Raise heat to high. Add wine to pot, stirring with a wooden spoon to deglaze. Add the stock, sauerkraut, poultry, ham hock, juniper berries, peppercorns, thyme, cloves, and bay leaf. Stir together and bring to a simmer. Lower heat, cover, and cook, barely simmering, until meat is tender, about 1½ hours.

Recipe can be made to this point a day ahead.

COOKING AND SERVING: Add sausage and red potatoes to the pot, stirring carefully, and season to taste with salt and pepper. Continue to cook until potatoes are tender, about ½ hour. Remove and discard ham hock. Stir in reserved bacon. Adjust seasoning if necessary and serve.

YIELD: 4 servings

Pamela Parseghian
Food editor
COOK'S Magazine

Stuffed Vegetables Armenian Style

In this rendition of an Armenian favorite, the stuffing is partially cooked so that the vegetables require less cooking and remain a little more firm.

PREPARING VEGETABLES FOR STUFFING

Begin with firm vegetables (especially tomatoes) so that they do not fall apart when you hollow them out. If you don't have a melon baller to scoop out the zucchini, a grapefruit spoon also works well. Be careful not to overstuff the vegetables since the rice mixture will continue to cook, and therefore expand, as the vegetables simmer.

INGREDIENTS

- 2 **tomatoes**
- 2 **red bell peppers**
- 2 **green bell peppers**
- 4 **zucchini**
- 1 **head savoy or regular cabbage**

Beef and Lamb Stuffing

- 3 **tomatoes**
- 3 **onions**
- 1½ **tablespoons olive oil**
- ½ **cup rice**
- **Salt and pepper**
- ¼ **cup chopped parsley**
- ⅔ **pound ground beef**
- ⅔ **pound ground lamb**
- ½ **teaspoon cayenne**

- 2 **lemons**
- ½ **cup parsley stems**

METHOD

PREPARATION: Cut a ¾-inch slice from the top of the tomatoes. Scoop out the insides, leaving only the outside wall. Discard the seeds and set the pulp aside. Cut a ¾-inch slice from the top of the bell peppers and remove and discard seeds and ribs. Halve zucchini crosswise. With a small melon baller or a thin, small spoon, hollow out the zucchini, leaving a thin wall of flesh. Discard seeds and pulp. Cut cabbage leaves away from the core and trim tough stems from leaves.

For the stuffing, peel, seed, and chop the 3 tomatoes. Mince the onions. Heat olive oil over medium-high heat and stir in the rice and 1½ teaspoons salt. Sauté until golden, about 2 minutes. Stir in the onions and cook until they begin to soften, about 3 minutes. Add the chopped tomatoes and reserved pulp and cook, stirring frequently, until juices are reduced, about 5 minutes. Put in a large bowl and cool.

Chop the parsley. Add beef, lamb, 3 tablespoons of the parsley, the cayenne, and about 1½ teaspoons salt to rice mixture. Combine well. Season insides of vegetables with salt and black pepper. Fill all of the vegetables loosely with the beef and lamb stuffing. Put "lids" on top of the tomatoes and peppers. Wrap the remaining stuffing in cabbage leaves. Put about ¼ cup stuffing near the bottom of each cabbage leaf. Roll partially, fold in sides, and roll up completely. Squeeze ¼ cup juice from the lemons.

Recipe can be made to this point several hours ahead.

COOKING AND SERVING: Line the bottom of a large pot with parsley stems and the remaining cabbage. Add lemon juice, 1 cup water, and about ¾ teaspoon salt. Put the peppers and zucchini on the bottom (reassembled with cut sides together) and the tomatoes and cabbage rolls on top. Put a small, heavy dish on top of the vegetables to keep them from floating and cover the pot.

Bring to a simmer and cook over low heat until just done, about 30 minutes. Remove and serve. Add remaining chopped parsley to cooking liquid and serve on the side.

YIELD: 4 servings

Pamela Parseghian
Food editor
COOK'S Magazine

VINCENT LEE

Chicken Pot Pie

This old favorite makes a triumphant return to the American table, spiffed up with wild mushrooms and a little tarragon.

INGREDIENTS

	Short Crust, recipe follows
½	ounce dried chanterelles
2	tablespoons minced fresh parsley
1	tablespoon minced fresh tarragon *or* 1 teaspoon dried tarragon
2	shallots
6 to 8	scallions
8	large fresh mushrooms (about 3 ounces)
1	cup baby carrots *or* 1 carrot
9	tablespoons butter, approximately
1	cup fresh *or* frozen baby green peas
1¼	pounds boneless, skinless chicken thighs
	Salt and pepper
3	tablespoons flour + more for coating chicken
3	cups chicken stock (page 30)
½	cup heavy cream
1	tablespoon cornstarch, if necessary
1	egg yolk, optional

METHOD

PREPARATION: Make the Short Crust. Reconstitute the dried mushrooms in ½ cup warm water. Chop reconstituted mushrooms. Strain the soaking water through a sieve lined with several layers of cheesecloth or a coffee filter. Mince the parsley, tarragon, and shallots. Cut the scallions into ½-inch pieces. Slice the fresh mushrooms. Slice the carrot, if using a large one. Cook carrots over medium heat in 1 tablespoon of the butter and 3 tablespoons water until tender, about 8 minutes. Blanch the fresh peas in boiling, salted water until tender, about 5 minutes. Drain, rinse under cold water, and drain again.

Cut chicken thighs in half. Season with salt and pepper, coat with flour, and shake off excess.

In a frying pan, sauté thighs in remaining 8 tablespoons of butter over medium heat until browned, turning often, about 10 minutes. Add shallots and fresh mushrooms and sauté a few minutes. Remove mixture from pan with a slotted spoon. Stir in the 3 tablespoons of flour, adding more butter if needed to absorb it, and cook 3 minutes. Pour in stock and stir over medium heat until smooth. Add dried, reconstituted mushrooms, reserved soaking liquid, and the cream to the sauce. It should be the consistency of medium white sauce. If it seems too thin, mix together a thick paste of cold water and cornstarch. Stir into the very center of the mixture over medium-low heat, using only enough of the paste to achieve proper consistency.

Return chicken and mushroom mixture to the sauce. Add carrots, peas, parsley, tarragon, and scallions. Pour chicken and vegetables into a deep pie pan or shallow soufflé dish.

On a floured work surface, roll out pastry to about ⅛-inch thick and center it over the pie. Flute the edges over the rim of the dish. Decorate with a pastry cut-out if desired. For a glossy crust, beat an egg yolk with 1 teaspoon water and brush egg wash over crust. Cut a few steam vents.

Recipe can be completed to this point several hours ahead.

COOKING: Heat oven to 400°F. Bake pie in preheated oven until golden brown, about 20 minutes.

YIELD: 4 servings

Short Crust

INGREDIENTS

1¼	cups flour
1	teaspoon salt
6	tablespoons cold lard or shortening
3	tablespoons cold water, approximately

METHOD

PREPARATION: Combine flour and salt. Cut lard into flour with a pastry blender or work it with your fingers. Add just enough cold water to hold the dough together, mixing with a fork. Form the dough into a ball, flatten, and wrap it in plastic. Chill for at least 15 minutes or even overnight.

YIELD: crust for 1 pot pie

Miriam Ungerer
Free-lance writer
Sag Harbor, NY

Sole and Vegetables in Papillote

You can use many different types of fish, depending on availability, including sole, pompano, snapper, or salmon, but thicker fillets should be sliced to a thickness of ¼ inch so that the fish cooks rapidly.

INGREDIENTS

2	**carrots**
2	**parsnips**
1	**small celery root**
2	**leeks**
12	**snow peas**
¼	**pound domestic or wild mushrooms**
6	**ounces fresh spinach**
4	**tablespoons butter or olive oil**
¼	**cup chopped fresh herbs, such as basil, thyme, and/or tarragon**
1½	**pounds fillet of sole or other fish fillet, such as salmon, snapper, or pompano**
	Salt and pepper
¼	**cup white wine, dry vermouth, or dry sherry**

Saffron Butter Sauce

⅓	**cup white wine**
3	**shallots**
¼	**teaspoon saffron threads**
¼	**cup heavy cream**
6	**ounces butter**
	Salt and pepper
⅛	**teaspoon cayenne pepper**

METHOD

PREPARATION: Cut the carrots, parsnips, and celery root into julienne strips. Trim the leeks, cut in quarters down to the root end, rinse thoroughly under cold water, and cut into julienne strips, including half of the green. Trim and string the snow peas. Blanch vegetables in boiling, salted water, about 15 seconds. Rinse under cold water and drain. Cut mushrooms into thin slices. Cut spinach into thin shreds. Melt the butter. Chop the herbs.

To assemble the papillotes, cut four 12- by 24-inch sheets of parchment paper or foil into large heart shapes or ovals and put them, shiny side down if using foil, on your work surface. Crease lengthwise to mark the center. Brush sheets lightly with a little of the melted butter or olive oil. Put a mound of spinach below the crease of each papillote. Cut the fish into 4 portions. Arrange the sole fillets on top of the spinach mounds and sprinkle with salt and black pepper and about ½ of the chopped herbs. Top with vegetables and mushrooms. Sprinkle on more salt and black pepper and the remaining fresh herbs, followed by the remaining butter or oil, and the ¼ cup wine.

Fold the top half of each papillote over the fish, bringing the edges together. Seal each pouch by folding over the edges, about ¼ inch at a time. Make the folds as neat and tight as possible to keep in the steam.

Mince the shallots.

Papillotes can be completed to this point several hours ahead.

COOKING AND SERVING: Heat oven to 400°F.

For the Saffron Butter Sauce, combine the ⅓ cup wine, shallots, and saffron in a heavy saucepan. Bring mixture to a boil and cook until the mixture is reduced to about 3 tablespoons of liquid. Add cream and boil until the mixture is reduced by half.

Bake the papillotes on baking sheets until puffed like balloons, 10 to 12 minutes. If you are using parchment paper, try not to open the oven while cooking (or open it just a crack) since cold air will make the puffs collapse.

Over low heat, whisk the butter, one piece at a time, into the reduced wine and cream mixture. The butter should not melt completely but should soften to form a creamy sauce. Season with salt, black pepper, and cayenne pepper, so that it is quite spicy.

Serve the papillotes closed so that each diner can enjoy the aroma as the papillote is opened. Pass the Saffron Butter Sauce separately.

YIELD: 4 servings

COOKING IN PAPILLOTE

Papillote is a parchment paper or foil pouch used for cooking fish, meat, or vegetables. The advantages to this cooking method are many: the pouches can be prepared ahead of time and refrigerated until ready to serve; vegetables and fish or meat can be cooked all at once in the pouch; actual cooking time is rapid; and the pouch seals in moistness, flavor and aroma. Add to this the fact that it makes a beautiful, dramatic presentation, and you have an ideal meal for a dinner party.

Steven Raichlen
Restaurant critic
Boston Magazine

Mayonnaise

INGREDIENTS

  1 **egg yolk**
  2 **teaspoons white-wine vinegar**
  ½ **teaspoon mustard, optional**
      Salt and pepper
  ⅔ **cup oil, such as peanut or olive oil**

METHOD

PREPARATION: In a small bowl, whisk the egg yolk with the vinegar, mustard, and ½ teaspoon salt. Whisk in the oil, drop by drop at first and then, when the sauce has emulsified, in a slow, thin stream. Season to taste with salt and pepper.

    Mayonnaise can be made several days ahead.

YIELD: about ⅔ cup

For the Mayonnaise, *whisk the egg mixture until thickened and then add the oil in a thin stream, whisking constantly.*

HOW TO MAKE PERFECT MAYONNAISE

Make sure to have all the ingredients at room temperature, or you may have trouble with the mayonnaise breaking. You can speed things up by putting the eggs in warm water to bring to room temperature. While mustard is an optional ingredient, it does help to facilitate the emulsification of the oil. As a general rule, one egg yolk can absorb ¾ cup of oil; any more and the mixture may break.

If the mayonnaise does curdle, it can be reconstituted by putting a teaspoon each of vinegar and mustard in a clean bowl. Add the "broken" mayonnaise a teaspoon at a time, whisking constantly until all the mayonnaise has been restored to creamy smoothness.

PASTA AND RICE

Ham and Three-Cheese Pasta Roll

Vivid colors make this rich pasta creation as beautiful as it is delicious.

ROLLING PASTA

While purists may claim that hand-rolled pasta is far superior to machine-rolled pasta, the amount of time, space, and brute strength required to roll pasta by hand make using a hand-cranked machine considerably more practical.

Divide the dough into 3 or 4 even pieces. Flatten slightly. Feeding the dough into the machine at a 45° angle, roll through several times until the dough is smooth and rectangular. Make sure you keep the dough as straight as possible as you feed it through, or it may wrinkle or tear.

Sarah Belk
Food editor
House Beautiful

INGREDIENTS

1 **recipe Spinach Pasta (page 66)**

Tomato Sauce
¼ **cup chopped fresh parsley**
2 **cloves garlic**
2 **tablespoons minced fresh basil *or* 2 teaspoons dried basil**
1 **pound canned Italian plum tomatoes**
3 **tablespoons butter**

Filling
4 **scallions**
2 **ounces smoked ham**
2 **tablespoons butter**
1 **ounce Parmesan cheese (about ¼ cup grated)**
½ **pound softened cream cheese**
4 **ounces whole-milk ricotta cheese (about ½ cup)**
1 **egg**
 Pepper

½ **pound thin-sliced ham**

METHOD

PREPARATION: Make the pasta dough.

For the Tomato Sauce, chop the parsley. Halve the garlic. Mince the basil. Drain the tomatoes. Put tomatoes, parsley, garlic, and basil in a saucepan. Break up the tomatoes with a large spoon. Simmer, uncovered, until reduced by ⅓, 30 to 40 minutes. The sauce should be thick. Strain, pressing firmly to get all the sauce. Return to the saucepan.

For the filling, mince the scallions. Cut the 2 ounces ham into ⅛-inch dice. Melt the 2 tablespoons butter in a frying pan. Add the scallions and cook over low heat until soft, 1 to 2 minutes. Add the diced ham and cook over medium heat for 1 to 2 minutes.

Grate the Parmesan cheese. In a bowl, beat the cream cheese and ricotta together until smooth. Add the egg and beat well. Stir in the Parmesan cheese, ham mixture, and pepper to taste. Mix well and refrigerate.

Recipe can be completed to this point several days ahead.

Roll the pasta out into four 12- by 4-inch sheets. Lay 2 of the pasta sheets side by side. Score 1 long edge with short diagonal strokes using the dull side of a knife. Brush water over the scoring. Lay the second sheet over the moistened edge to overlap by ½ inch. Press along the seam so that the sheets adhere.

Spread half of the filling over the assembled sheets of pasta, leaving a ½-inch border all the way around. Cover the filling with half the sliced ham. Beginning at one of the short ends, roll the pasta up tightly so that water cannot seep in as it poaches. Repeat the entire procedure with the remaining 2 sheets of pasta, filling, and ham, making 2 completed rolls. Wrap each roll in a double thickness of 12-inch square cheesecloth and tie each end securely with string.

Recipe can be completed to this point several hours ahead.

COOKING AND SERVING: Bring a large pot of salted water to a boil and add the pasta rolls. Reduce heat and simmer the rolls, turning them occasionally, for 25 minutes. Drain, cool slightly, and remove the string and cheesecloth.

Warm the tomato sauce and swirl in the 3 tablespoons butter.

Cut each pasta roll into ½-inch-thick slices. Pour tomato sauce onto plates and top with the pasta slices.

YIELD: 4 servings

Pasta with Broccoli Raab Pesto

This pleasingly pungent "pesto" is an unusual way to show off the flavor of broccoli raab.

INGREDIENTS

- 1½ **pounds broccoli raab (about 3 small bunches)**
- 8 **cloves garlic**
- 1 **ounce Parmesan cheese (about ¼ cup grated)**
- 7 **pickled *or* salt-packed anchovy fillets**
- ¼ **cup red-wine vinegar, approximately**
- 1 **cup extra-virgin olive oil + 2 tablespoons, if necessary**
- **Salt and pepper**
- ¾ **pound dry pasta shells**

METHOD

PREPARATION: Trim large stems and leaves from broccoli raab leaving small stems, leaves, and flower buds intact. Mince the garlic and broccoli raab by hand or in a food processor. Grate the cheese. If using salt-packed anchovy fillets, rinse them in water and then in a bit of red-wine vinegar.

Heat 1 cup of olive oil in a frying pan and sauté the broccoli raab and garlic until wilted, 3 to 4 minutes. Add ⅔ cup water, cover, and cook until broccoli raab is tender but still green, about 5 minutes more. Puree the mixture with the anchovy fillets in a food processor, blender, or through the fine plate of a food mill until very smooth, adding up to 2 more tablespoons of oil if necessary. Add the grated Parmesan cheese. Season to taste with salt and pepper and a dash of red-wine vinegar. Use just enough vinegar to bring out the flavor; the pesto should not taste vinegary.

Pesto can be made a day ahead.

COOKING AND SERVING: Cook the pasta in a large pot of boiling, salted water until just tender. Drain well and toss with the pesto. Season to taste with salt and pepper.

YIELD: 4 servings

Alice Waters
Owner
Chez Panisse and Cafe Fanny
Berkeley, CA

Olive Pasta

This simple tangle of pasta and sliced olives makes a lovely first course or light meal.

INGREDIENTS

- 1 **recipe Egg Pasta (page 66)** *or* **Spinach Pasta (page 66)** *or* **½ pound dry pasta, such as linguine, bavettine, or perciatelli**
- 1 **small red bell pepper**
- 1 **clove garlic**
  Salt and coarse black pepper
- 1½ **cups sliced Mediterranean black olives**
- ½ **cup sliced green olives**
- 6 **scallion tops**
- 1½ **tablespoons olive oil**

METHOD

PREPARATION: Make the pasta dough, rolling dough as thin as possible. Cut the dough into thin strips.

Roast the red pepper under the broiler, over a gas flame, or on a grill until blackened. Remove the skin and seeds and cut the flesh into ¼-inch dice. Crush the garlic with a pinch of salt. Slice the black and green olives. Chop the green scallion tops.

Recipe can be made to this point several hours ahead.

COOKING: Cook the pasta in a large pot of boiling, salted water until just tender. Drain.

Heat the oil in a large frying pan over medium heat. Add the garlic, stir, and then add the olives. Add the pasta and heat through. Toss the pasta with the scallion tops and red bell pepper and season to taste with salt and pepper.

YIELD: 4 servings

Sandra Matsukawa Hu
Free-lance writer
San Francisco, CA

Tagliatelle with Smoked Salmon and Asparagus

Smoked salmon and asparagus are a tantalizing duo in this quick pasta dish.

INGREDIENTS

1	recipe Egg Pasta (page 66) *or* ½ pound flat, dry pasta, such as tagliatelle
¾	pound thin asparagus
¾	pound smoked salmon with skin
1½	shallots
6	ounces butter
¾	cup white wine
1	lemon
2½	cups heavy cream
1½	teaspoons canned green peppercorns
	Salt and pepper

METHOD

PREPARATION: Make the pasta dough. Roll it as thin as possible and cut into ½-inch-wide strips. Trim the asparagus and blanch in a large pot of boiling, salted water until just tender, about 7 minutes. Drain, plunge into cold water, and drain again. Skin and cut the salmon on an angle into ½-inch strips. Reserve skin. Chop the shallots.

Melt the butter in a frying pan, add the shallots, and sauté until soft, about 3 minutes. Add the wine and squeeze in 2 tablespoons of lemon juice. Stir with a wooden spoon to deglaze the bottom of the pan, and cook over medium-high heat until reduced by ½, about 3 minutes. Add the salmon skin and heavy cream. Cook over medium heat until slightly thickened, about 10 minutes. Strain.

Recipe can be made to this point several hours ahead.

COOKING: Cook the pasta in a large pot of boiling, salted water until tender. Drain and return to pot. Add sauce, salmon, asparagus spears, and green peppercorns. Toss, heat through over low heat, and season to taste with salt and pepper.

YIELD: 4 servings

Peter Morency
Chef
Nob Hill Restaurant
San Francisco, CA

Green and White Pasta with Peas and Pancetta

RICHARD FELBER

Salty pancetta contrasts nicely with sweet peas in this cream-drenched pasta.

SWEET PEAS

Peas, like sweet corn, have a high sugar content that converts rapidly to starch after being picked. Therefore, garden-fresh peas are a true delicacy. They're worth shopping the farm stands for, or even growing your own.

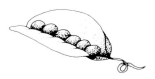

INGREDIENTS

- ½ recipe Egg Pasta (page 66) *or* 4 ounces dry, flat pasta, such as fettuccine
- ½ recipe Spinach Pasta (page 66) *or* 4 ounces dry, flat spinach pasta, such as fettuccine
- 4 to 6 ounces thick-sliced pancetta
- 1 pound fresh peas (about 1½ cups or 7 ounces shelled)
- 1 cup heavy cream
- Salt
- Lemon juice, optional

METHOD

PREPARATION: Make the Egg and Spinach Pasta doughs. Roll each dough as thin as possible. Cut into ⅛- to ¼-inch-wide strips.

Cut pancetta into ½-inch pieces. Shell peas. Blanch peas in boiling, salted water for about 5 minutes. Drain and refresh under cold water.

Recipe can be made to this point several hours ahead.

COOKING AND SERVING: Cook pancetta in a large frying pan until fat is rendered. Pour off fat. Add cream and peas to the pancetta and heat gently.

Cook both pastas in a pot of boiling, salted water until just tender. Drain and then put pasta directly into pan with peas and cream. Toss all ingredients together and season to taste with salt and lemon juice if desired.

YIELD: 4 servings

Alice Waters
Owner
Chez Panisse and Café
  Fanny
Berkeley, CA

Chicken and Pasta with Jalapeno and Tomato Dressing

This herb-and-jalapeno-zapped tomato dressing tastes fresh and pungent. Topping the pasta is crisp, crusty, cumin-spiced chicken.

INGREDIENTS

- 2 cloves garlic
- 1 tablespoon minced fresh ginger
- 2 teaspoons ground cumin
- 3 tablespoons red-wine vinegar
- ¼ cup olive oil
- Salt and pepper
- 8 chicken thighs (about 2 pounds total)

Jalapeno and Tomato Dressing

- 4 tomatoes
- 2 jalapenos or other fresh, hot chili peppers
- 2 cloves garlic
- 1 small red onion
- 1 cup minced fresh mint
- 1 cup minced fresh coriander
- 2 tablespoons red-wine vinegar
- 2 tablespoons olive oil
- Salt and pepper

- ½ pound fusilli or other dry pasta
- Mint and/or coriander sprigs for garnish, optional

METHOD

PREPARATION: Mince the garlic and ginger. In a bowl, combine the garlic, ginger, cumin, the 3 tablespoons vinegar, the ¼ cup olive oil, and salt and pepper to taste. Add the chicken, stir to coat, and let stand at room temperature, stirring once or twice, for about 1½ hours.

For the Jalapeno and Tomato Dressing, peel, seed, and chop the tomatoes and put into a large bowl. Seed and mince the jalapenos. Mince the garlic and onion. Mince the mint and coriander. Add the garlic, onion, jalapenos, mint, and coriander to the bowl with the tomatoes. Stir in 2 tablespoons vinegar, 2 tablespoons olive oil, and salt to taste and let stand at room temperature, stirring once or twice, for at least 45 minutes.

Recipe can be made to this point a few hours ahead.

COOKING AND SERVING: Heat the grill. If using wood chips, soak a handful in water for 20 minutes. Put chips on the fire. Grill the chicken, turning occasionally and brushing with the marinade, until crisp and dark brown on both sides, about 15 minutes total. Or broil for about 20 minutes.

Cook the pasta in a large pot of boiling, salted water until just tender. Drain and toss immediately with the tomato dressing.

Season pasta to taste with salt and pepper and put onto plates. Top each serving with 2 grilled chicken thighs and garnish with mint and/or coriander sprigs. Serve warm.

YIELD: 4 servings

Michael McLaughlin
Chef/owner
The Manhattan Chili Company
New York, NY

Fedelini with Duck, Grapes, and Cracked Peppercorns

Sweet and sour sauce enlivens this unusual dish; cracked peppercorns add a nice bite.

INGREDIENTS

1 **5-pound duck**
  Salt and pepper
1 **recipe Egg Pasta (page 66)** *or* **½ pound flat, dry pasta, such as fedelini or vermicelli**

Duck Stock

1 **onion**
1 **small carrot**
  Carcass from duck, above
½ **cup red wine**
6 **cups veal stock or chicken stock (page 30) or a combination of stock and water**

Sweet and Sour Sauce

2 **shallots**
1 **tablespoon crushed black peppercorns**
1 **orange**
1 **lemon**
1 **tablespoon butter**
¼ **cup red wine**
2 **cups duck stock, above**
1½ **tablespoons red-currant jelly**
1 **tablespoon port**

1 **cup seedless red grapes**
2 **tablespoons Dijon mustard**
  Salt

METHOD

PREPARATION: Heat oven to 450°F. Remove the giblets from the duck and discard. Cut off the last 2 wing joints and put them into a roasting pan with the duck neck. Dry the duck with paper towels and prick all over with a fork. Rub inside and out with salt and pepper. Put duck on top of the wing joints and neck. Roast for 20 minutes. Reduce heat to 300°F and continue roasting for 2 hours, straining off fat as it accumulates. Remove the duck from the oven and set aside to cool. When cool remove all the meat and skin. Cut the meat into strips about 1½ inches long and ¼-inch thick. Reserve meat, skin, bones, and the roasting pan.

Make the pasta dough, rolling dough out as thin

as possible. Cut the dough in ⅛-inch wide strips or as thin as possible.

For the Duck Stock, chop the onion and carrot. Chop the duck bones, including the neck and wing tips, into pieces and put into a stockpot. Pour off the fat from the roasting pan and set it over high heat. Add the wine, scraping the bottom of the pan with a wooden spoon to deglaze. Add this liquid to the stockpot with the onion, carrot, and the 6 cups stock. Bring to a boil, reduce heat, and simmer, skimming as necessary, until reduced to 3 cups, 2 to 3 hours. Strain and skim well to degrease. Reduce stock over medium heat to about 2 cups, 15 to 20 minutes. Set aside.

For the sauce, mince the shallots. Crush the peppercorns. Squeeze 2 tablespoons juice each from the orange and lemon. Melt the butter in a large frying pan. Add the shallots, cook over low heat for 3 minutes, and add the wine. Turn heat to high and reduce to 2 to 3 tablespoons, about 10 minutes. Add the reserved duck stock, jelly, port, and orange and lemon juices. Continue to boil gently until the liquid is reduced by half and is slightly syrupy, 20 to 25 minutes.

Recipe can be made to this point a day ahead.

Heat oven to 350°F. Put the reserved duck skin on a baking sheet and cook in preheated oven until browned and crisp, about 30 minutes. Sprinkle with salt, drain on paper towels, and cool. Break into small pieces. Halve the grapes.

Recipe can be made to this point several hours ahead.

COOKING AND SERVING: Cook the pasta in a large pot of boiling, salted water until tender and then drain.

Reheat the sauce if necessary. Add the duck strips and fedelini to the sauce and toss. Cook until just heated through, 3 to 5 minutes. Add grape halves to the sauce along with the crushed peppercorns and mustard. Season with salt and toss well.

Serve sprinkled with the crisp skin.

YIELD: 4 servings

Sara Moulton
Editor, food department
Gourmet Magazine

Oriental Pilaf with Peaches

This lovely, slightly sweet side dish puts juicy summer peaches to good use.

INGREDIENTS

2	tablespoons slivered almonds
6	snow peas
1	lime
1½	teaspoons chopped fresh ginger
1	scallion
1	peach
2	tablespoons butter
1	cup long-grain white rice
	Salt and pepper

METHOD

PREPARATION: Heat oven to 350°F. Spread the almonds in a shallow baking pan and toast, stirring once or twice, until lightly browned, about 5 minutes. Cool.

Trim and string the peas and cook in boiling, salted water until tender, about 1 minute. Drain, refresh under cold water, and drain again. Cut peas diagonally into ½-inch pieces.

Grate zest from lime. Squeeze 2 tablespoons lime juice. Mince the ginger. Slice the scallion.

Recipe can be made to this point 1 hour ahead.

COOKING AND SERVING: Peel, pit and dice the peach. Heat 1 tablespoon of the butter in a saucepan over medium heat until foamy. Add the diced peach and sauté, stirring gently until lightly softened, about 2 minutes. Remove and reserve.

In the same pan, melt the remaining tablespoon of butter, add the scallion, and sauté until softened, about 2 minutes. Add the ginger and cook 1 minute longer. Add the rice, stirring to coat with the butter, and cook 1 minute. Stir in 2 cups of water, the lime zest, and lime juice. Bring the liquid just to a boil over high heat. Lower heat, cover, and simmer until the liquid is absorbed and the rice is tender, about 20 minutes.

Stir in the almonds, snow peas, and sautéed peach.

Season to taste with salt and pepper and serve.

YIELD: 4 servings

Elizabeth Riely
Free-lance writer
Newton Centre, MA

Risotto with Artichokes

Creamy risotto, flavored with Parmesan, makes a satisfying first course or a nice light meal.

ABOUT RISOTTO

Risotto is a rice preparation commonly used in Italy for which you saute the rice and then add liquid little by little, stirring all the while. Making risotto requires a fair amount of attention since some types of rice absorb liquid more quickly or cook more slowly than others. The final product should be tender, but still whole, grains in a creamy-textured sauce. Risotto is best made with arborio rice, which is shorter and rounder than American short-grained rice, but if unavailable, any short-grained or even long-grained rice will do.

INGREDIENTS

1	clove garlic
¼	cup chopped fresh flat-leaf parsley
1	ounce Parmesan cheese (about ¼ cup grated)
½	lemon
1	large artichoke or 2 smaller artichokes
6	tablespoons olive oil
3	cups chicken stock (page 30)
	Salt and pepper
½	small onion
¾	cup arborio or other rice
⅔	cup white wine
2	tablespoons butter

METHOD

PREPARATION: Slice the garlic as thin as possible. Chop the parsley. Grate the cheese. Squeeze juice from lemon.

Snap off the artichoke stem and remove the tough outer leaves until only pale yellow inner leaves remain. Cut the artichoke in half lengthwise, and cut out the fuzzy choke. Use a grapefruit spoon or teaspoon to dig out the fuzzy fibers and then wipe the heart clean. Rub the artichoke at once with lemon juice to prevent discoloration. Slice each artichoke half as thin as possible crosswise and toss with lemon juice.

In a saucepan, heat 3 tablespoons of the oil. Sauté the artichoke slices and garlic over medium heat until the garlic is soft, about 3 minutes. Add ⅓ cup of the chicken stock, 3 tablespoons of the parsley, and pepper to taste. Simmer until the artichoke is just tender, about 30 minutes. Chop the onion.

Recipe can be made to this point several hours ahead.

COOKING AND SERVING: Heat the remaining 3 tablespoons of oil in a separate saucepan. Cook the onion until soft, about 3 minutes. Add the rice and stir for 1 minute to coat. Stir in the wine. Cook, stirring, over medium-high heat until most of the wine has evaporated, about 4 minutes.

Heat the remaining stock and add about ⅔ cup to the rice. Cook, stirring continuously, until all the liquid has been absorbed.

Stir the artichoke mixture into the risotto. Add more stock, ⅓ cup at a time, stirring continuously. Wait until most of the liquid has been absorbed before adding more stock. When all the stock has been used, the grains should be soft but still whole and the remaining liquid thickened to a creamy consistency, about 20 minutes. Stir in the butter and 3 tablespoons of the cheese. Season with salt and pepper to taste.

Serve the risotto at once, sprinkled with the remaining cheese and parsley.

YIELD: 4 servings

Pat Opler
Owner/instructor
Home on the Range
  Cooking School
Wilson, WY

Wild Rice and Apple Griddle Cakes

An old-fashioned favorite gets dressed for dinner.

INGREDIENTS

- ⅓ cup wild rice
- ¼ cup flour
- 1 tablespoon baking powder
- 1½ teaspoons brown sugar
  Salt and pepper
- ¾ cup yellow cornmeal
- 2 scallions or 1 small onion
- 2 tablespoons chopped pecans
- 2 small, tart apples
- 3 tablespoons butter
- 1 egg
- ½ cup milk

METHOD

PREPARATION: Cook the wild rice in boiling, salted water, partly covered, until tender, about 40 minutes. Drain and rinse under cold water. Chop. Sift together flour, baking powder, brown sugar, and 1 teaspoon salt. Stir in the cornmeal.

Mince the scallions. Chop the pecans. Peel, core, and dice the apples. Heat the butter in a large frying pan over medium heat. Add the wild rice, scallions, pecans, and apples. Season with salt and pepper and sauté lightly for 2 to 3 minutes. Cool.

Recipe can be made to this point several hours ahead.

COOKING AND SERVING: Lightly beat the egg, add to dry ingredients along with the milk, and stir until batter is smooth. Add rice mixture.

Butter and heat a griddle or heavy frying pan over medium heat. Drop batter by the tablespoon onto the griddle or frying pan. Turn when tiny holes form in each cake and cook until golden, about 5 minutes total. Cook in batches if necessary.

Keep cooked griddle cakes warm in a low oven while the rest are completed. Serve immediately.

YIELD: 4 servings

THE VERSATILE GRIDDLE CAKE

Once used only to lure lazy-bones out of bed, the griddle cake isn't just for breakfast any more. Try these savory cakes as an accompaniment for grilled or roasted poultry. Of course, with a little maple syrup or apple sauce, these griddle cakes will still bring the latest of sleepers to the table.

Larry Forgione
Chef/owner
An American Place
New York, NY

Egg Pasta

INGREDIENTS

2 cups flour
1 teaspoon salt
2 eggs

METHOD

PREPARATION: Mix flour and salt in a bowl and make a well in the center. Beat the eggs and pour into the well. With fingertips or a fork, mix flour and eggs together gently until the dough begins to stick together, about 3 minutes. Add up to 2 tablespoons of water if needed. When the dough comes together in a mass, turn it out onto a lightly floured work surface and knead until satiny and resilient, 10 to 15 minutes. Wrap in plastic wrap and set aside to rest for at least 45 minutes.

Egg pasta can be refrigerated for up to 3 days, or it can be frozen.

YIELD: ¾ pound Egg Pasta

FREEZING HOMEMADE PASTA

You can freeze uncooked, rolled, and cut pasta by first spreading it out on a baking sheet and freezing until solid and then removing and wrapping well in plastic. Don't defrost—drop right into boiling, salted water. It will take only slightly longer to cook than fresh.

Spinach Pasta

INGREDIENTS

6 ounces fresh spinach (about 1½ quarts)
2 cups flour
1 teaspoon salt
2 eggs

METHOD

PREPARATION: Wash the spinach. Cook spinach in boiling, salted water until tender. Drain and squeeze out excess water. You should have about ⅓ cup cooked spinach. Mince the spinach.

Mix flour and salt in a bowl and make a well in the center. Beat eggs lightly. Add spinach to eggs and beat to combine. Pour into the well. With fingertips or a fork, mix flour and egg-spinach mixture together gently until the dough begins to stick together, about 3 minutes. Add up to 2 tablespoons water if needed. When the dough comes together in a mass, turn it out onto a lightly floured work surface and knead until satiny and resilient, 10 to 15 minutes. Wrap in plastic wrap and set aside to rest for at least 45 minutes.

Spinach Pasta can be refrigerated for up to 3 days or it can be frozen.

YIELD: ¾ pound Spinach Pasta

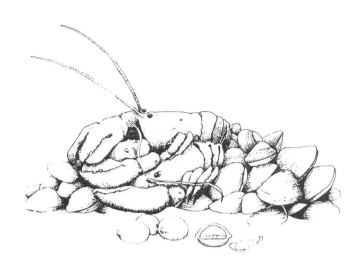

FISH AND SHELLFISH

Mexican-Style Mussels

Hot, spicy sausage adds fire to these unusual mussels; lime wedges provide cool relief.

INGREDIENTS

- 3 **pounds mussels**
- 3 **ears fresh corn** *or* **1½ cups frozen kernels**
- 9 **ounces chorizo**
- 4 **cloves garlic**
- 4 **oranges**
- 1 **lime**
- ¾ **cup chopped coriander**
- ⅓ **cup olive oil**
- ⅓ **cup dry white wine**
- **Salt and pepper**

METHOD

PREPARATION: Scrub and debeard mussels. Cook the fresh corn in boiling, salted water until tender, about 5 minutes. Cut the kernels from the cobs. You should have about 1½ cups corn kernels. Slice chorizo. Mince the garlic.

Squeeze 1 cup juice from the oranges. Put the orange juice in a nonreactive pan and reduce by half over high heat, about 6 minutes. Cut the lime into wedges. Chop coriander.

Recipe can be made to this point a few hours ahead.

COOKING AND SERVING: Heat the olive oil in a large, nonreactive pot over medium heat. Add the mussels and cook, covered, shaking occasionally, for 2 minutes. Add the garlic and chorizo and cook, stirring, about 1 minute. Add the wine and continue cooking until all the mussels open, about 2 minutes more.

Add the corn and orange juice and cook, stirring, until the corn is heated through, about 2 minutes. Add the coriander leaves and season with salt and pepper. Garnish with lime wedges.

YIELD: 4 servings

Robert Bell
Chef
Chez Melange
Redondo Beach, CA

Sausages and Oysters

Odd though this may sound, sausages and oysters is an old and venerable combination in French cuisine.

INGREDIENTS

2 dozen oysters
1 pound hot or sweet Italian sausages

METHOD

PREPARATION: Scrub the oysters.

COOKING: Heat the grill. Cook the sausages over a medium-hot bed of coals, turning frequently, until skin is crisp and sausages are just cooked through, about 10 minutes.

About 3 minutes before the sausages are done, put the oysters on the grill, deep shell down, cover, and cook until they open, about 3 minutes. Be careful when uncovering the grill; the shells sometimes pop.

YIELD: 4 servings

SERVING SUGGESTIONS FOR SAUSAGES AND OYSTERS

Larger varieties of oysters are better than small ones for this treatment, since they're easier to handle on a hot grill when roasted. Fried onions and sweet peppers, along with some Italian bread, are the best accompaniments for this meal. And try a full-flavored dark beer.

Miriam Ungerer
Free-lance writer
Sag Harbor, NY

RICHARD FELBER

Smoked Shrimp with Black-Bean Salad

SHRIMP FROM THE FARM

While farm-raised shrimp still claim only a tiny percentage of the market, aquaculture is surely the wave of the future. Demand keeps growing while the wild shrimp harvest remains the same. The good news: farm-raised shrimp are fresher, cleaner, and tastier than their wild brothers. The bad news: they're also more expensive.

Anne Byrn
Food editor and restaurant critic
The Atlanta Journal and
The Atlanta Constitution

RICHARD FELBER

Black beans, flecked with a confetti of red and green peppers, provide a beautiful backdrop for dusky pink, smoked shrimp.

INGREDIENTS

	Salt and pepper
24	large shrimp, in the shell
½	pound dried black beans
1	bay leaf
¼	cup chopped parsley + 2 sprigs
1	small onion
2	red bell peppers
2	green bell peppers
4	scallions
5	tablespoons olive oil
1	tomato

METHOD

PREPARATION: Dissolve 2 tablespoons of salt in 1 quart of water. Rinse shrimp and soak in the salted water, refrigerated, overnight. Soak the beans overnight in a large bowl with enough cold water to cover by at least 1 inch. Or, bring the beans just to a boil, remove from heat, and let sit, covered, for 1 hour.

Drain and rinse the beans and put in a pot with enough cold water to cover by at least 1 inch. Add the bay leaf, parsley sprigs, and onion and bring just to a boil. Reduce heat and simmer until beans are tender but not mushy, about 1½ hours. Remove and discard the bay leaf and onion. Drain beans.

Recipe can be made to this point a day ahead.

Dice the bell peppers and scallions. Chop the ¼ cup parsley.

Heat ¼ cup of the olive oil in a frying pan over medium-low heat, add the bell peppers, and sauté until soft, about 5 minutes. Add sautéed bell peppers, scallions, chopped parsley, and salt and pepper to taste to the beans.

Remove shrimp from the brine and pat dry.

Recipe can be made to this point several hours ahead.

COOKING AND SERVING: Peel, seed, and chop the tomato. Toss beans with remaining olive oil. The salad should be served at room temperature.

Heat a charcoal grill until coals turn ash gray. While grill heats, soak wood chips, such as apple or cherry, in water. Put a layer of chips on top of coals. Lay shrimp on grill about 6 inches above the coals, cover the grill, and cook, turning once, until shrimp are firm and just cooked through, about 15 minutes total. Remove from grill. Peel and devein.

Put bean salad on plates and sprinkle with chopped tomato. Arrange the shrimp around the salad.

YIELD: 4 servings

Shellfish Louisiana

For the Shellfish Louisiana, remove the lobster claw meat in one piece by first moving the "thumb" from side to side and pulling it off. Reserve the shell for the stock.

With the dull side of a large knife, hit the edge of the claw hard enough to crack the shell. Repeat on the opposite edge of the claw.

Gently slide the claw meat from the cracked shell.

You can choose your favorite shellfish for this luxurious first course.

INGREDIENTS

Croutons

5	slices white bread
2	tablespoons oil
2	tablespoons butter
2	pounds crayfish *or* 1 pound shrimp *or* one 1½-pound lobster *or* ½ pound crabmeat

Shellfish Stock

½	onion
½	rib celery
½	carrot
¼	pound shellfish shells
1	sprig parsley
2	peppercorns
2½	cups water
2	slices bacon
1	scallion
2	teaspoons minced parsley
2	tablespoons butter
2	tablespoons flour
½	cup heavy cream
¼	teaspoon hot red-pepper sauce
	Pinch thyme
	Pinch oregano
	Salt and pepper

METHOD

PREPARATION: *For the croutons,* remove the crust from the bread. Cut each slice in half crosswise and then each half into 2 triangles. Heat 1 tablespoon of the oil in a large frying pan over medium heat. Add 1 tablespoon of the butter and let melt. Fry half the triangles until golden on both sides. Heat remaining oil and butter and fry the rest of the triangles.

Croutons can be made a few days ahead and stored in an airtight container.

Bring a pot of water to a boil and add crayfish, shrimp or lobster. Return to a boil and cook crayfish for 30 seconds, shrimp for 1 minute, or lobster for 10 minutes. Drain and cool. If using crayfish, set aside 4 for garnish. Remove meat from shells, save shells for stock, and dice shrimp or lobster. Leave crayfish meat whole.

For the stock, put all ingredients in a large pot. Bring to a boil and skim foam that rises to the top. Lower heat and simmer, uncovered, for 2 hours. Strain. You should have about 1¼ cups of stock. Reduce by boiling or add water if you have more or less.

Dice the bacon. Mince the scallion and parsley.

Recipe can be made to this point several hours ahead.

COOKING AND SERVING: In a heavy saucepan, cook bacon over low heat until crisp, about 5 minutes. Remove bacon and pour out all but a thin film of fat. Raise heat to medium and add the 2 tablespoons butter. Sauté shellfish and scallion for 30 seconds. Remove with a slotted spoon. Add flour to frying pan and stir well. Cook roux over medium heat, stirring, until golden, about 3 minutes. Gradually stir in the 1¼ cups stock, cream, hot red-pepper sauce, thyme, oregano, and salt and pepper to taste. Bring to a boil and then simmer over medium heat, stirring often, for 2 minutes. Return bacon, shellfish, and scallion to frying pan and stir well. Taste for seasoning.

Arrange five croutons in a star pattern on each plate and put the shellfish in the center. Sprinkle with parsley and garnish with whole reserved crayfish if desired.

YIELD: 4 servings

Beverly Cox
Free-lance writer
Norwalk, CT

RICHARD FELBER

Bay Scallops with Lime and Mint

Sweet bay scallops are cooked without heat by marinating them in a zesty lime juice preparation. This delicious dish can be prepared several hours ahead.

COOKING WITHOUT HEAT

Marination originally referred only to salt curing. The Italian *marinare*, the French *mariner*, and the Spanish *marinar* all mean "of the sea" in reference to the brine in which the food is pickled. The addition of acids to the curing solution revolutionized the method by adding zesty flavor and inspiring new combinations. Salt and acid actually cook food in much the same way heat does—by breaking down tough, connective tissues and firming proteins.

Sara Moulton
Editor, food department
Gourmet Magazine

INGREDIENTS

¾ pound bay scallops
3 limes
    Salt and pepper
1 small red onion
1 small clove garlic
3 tablespoons chopped fresh mint, plus
    whole mint leaves for garnish
⅛ teaspoon cayenne pepper
5 tablespoons oil
2 small ripe avocados

METHOD

PREPARATION: Wash scallops with cold water and pat dry. Grate zest from lime. Squeeze 3 tablespoons plus 2 teaspoons lime juice. In a bowl, toss the scallops with ¼ teaspoon salt, 3 tablespoons of the lime juice, and grated zest. Cover and refrigerate. Marinate the scallops until they are firm and opaque, at least 6 hours, stirring occasionally.

Scallops can be prepared a day ahead.

Mince the onion. Soak in cold water for 20 minutes. Squeeze with your hands and set aside on a paper towel to dry. Mince the garlic. Chop the mint.

Recipe can be completed to this point a few hours ahead.

SERVING: Combine 1 teaspoon salt and remaining 2 teaspoons lime juice with the garlic, pepper to taste, and ⅛ teaspoon cayenne in a large bowl. Slowly whisk in the oil to make a dressing.

Drain the scallops and toss them with all but 2 tablespoons of the dressing, the onion, and chopped mint. Adjust the seasonings.

Peel and slice the avocados, arrange on individual serving plates, and drizzle the remaining dressing over them. Mound the scallops on the plates and garnish with fresh mint leaves.

YIELD: 4 servings

Sesame Sautéed Catfish with Lemon Butter

VINCENT LEE

Sesame seeds add crunch and parsley adds color to quickly sautéed catfish.

INGREDIENTS

- ½ cup + 1 tablespoon minced fresh parsley
- 1 cup dry bread crumbs
- ½ cup sesame seeds
  Salt and pepper
- ¼ cup flour
- 2 eggs
- 3 tablespoons butter
- 2 lemons
- 4 catfish fillets (about 1½ pounds total)
- 3 tablespoons peanut oil

METHOD

PREPARATION: Mince the parsley. In a shallow bowl, combine ½ cup of the parsley with bread crumbs, sesame seeds, and salt and pepper. Put flour in another shallow bowl. In a third shallow bowl, beat eggs with 1 teaspoon water.

To make lemon butter, melt butter and squeeze in 1 tablespoon lemon juice from one of the lemons. Cut remaining lemon into 4 wedges and dip edges into remaining tablespoon of parsley.

Recipe can be prepared to this point several hours ahead.

COOKING AND SERVING: Dredge each fillet in the flour and then dip in beaten eggs. Coat with bread crumb/sesame seed mixture. Reheat lemon butter if necessary.

Heat the oil in a frying pan over medium heat until hot. Sauté coated fillets, turning once, until each side is well browned and fish just tests done, 3 to 5 minutes per side. Put fillets on warm plates, garnish with lemon, and pass lemon butter separately.

YIELD: 4 servings

Anne Byrn
Food editor and restaurant
  critic
The Atlanta Journal and
The Atlanta Constitution

Trout with Herb Butter Sauce

RICHARD FELBER

*Fresh herbs add their distinctive but subtle flavor
to a delicate butter sauce, perfectly suited to tender
poached trout fillets.*

MAKING THE SAUCE

The Herb Butter Sauce used here is a variation of the traditional French beurre blanc. Rich and flavorful, the sauce is also subtle enough so that it won't overpower the delicate taste of poached fish.

The trick to making this sauce is to emulsify the butter without melting it so that the sauce is creamy. The acid in the wine and vinegar will aid emulsification. Whisk in cold butter, a tablespoon at a time, over the lowest possible heat, moving on and off the heat as necessary.

INGREDIENTS

Court Bouillon

1	small carrot
1	small rib celery
½	yellow onion
3	sprigs fresh thyme *or* 1 teaspoon dried thyme
1	large sprig parsley
3	cups water
½	cup white wine
1½	teaspoons salt

Herb Butter Sauce

2	tablespoons minced chives
2	tablespoons minced parsley
2	tablespoons minced fresh tarragon *or* ½ teaspoon dried tarragon
¼	cup Court Bouillon, from above
¼	cup white wine
1	teaspoon white-wine vinegar
6	tablespoons butter
1	teaspoon lemon juice
	Salt and pepper

4	unskinned trout fillets or salmon-trout fillets (about 1½ pounds total)

METHOD

PREPARATION: *For the Court Bouillon,* peel the carrot and cut into thin slices. Cut celery and onion into thin slices. In a nonreactive pot, combine all ingredients, bring to a simmer, cover, and cook for 20 minutes. You should have about 3 cups.

Court Bouillon can be made several days ahead, or it can be frozen.

For the sauce, mince the chives, parsley, and tarragon. This can be done several hours ahead.

COOKING AND SERVING: Bring Court Bouillon to a simmer. Put the fillets, skin side down, into the simmering liquid, lower heat, and poach gently until fish is just cooked through, about 5 minutes. Remove fish from the liquid, peel off the skin, and cover to keep warm.

Strain the Court Bouillon and put ¼ cup of it into a small saucepan. Reserve remaining bouillon for another use. Add the wine and vinegar to the saucepan and bring to a boil until liquid is reduced to 2 tablespoons, about 3 minutes. Over the lowest possible heat, whisk in the butter a bit at a time. The butter should soften to form a creamy sauce but should not melt completely. Stir in the chives, parsley, tarragon, and lemon juice. Season to taste with salt and pepper.

Serve the fish topped with sauce.

YIELD: 4 servings

Melanie Barnard
Free-lance writer
New Canaan, CT

Panfried Lake Trout with Chili Hollandaise

Larry Forgione, chef/owner of An American Place, created this spiced-up version of the classic hollandaise to go with panfried fish.

INGREDIENTS

Chili Hollandaise

1   small onion
1   clove garlic
¼   cup minced red bell pepper
2   tablespoons minced green bell pepper
1   tablespoon butter
3   tablespoons chili powder
    Salt and pepper
½   teaspoon cayenne pepper
¼   teaspoon dried oregano
¼   cup dry white wine
1   cup fish stock or chicken stock
    (page 30)
    Hollandaise Sauce (page 82)

Panfried Lake Trout

1   cup sour cream
½   cup buttermilk
½   teaspoon hot red-pepper sauce
4   teaspoons spicy mustard
2   egg yolks
    Salt and pepper
1   cup flour
½   cup stone-ground cornmeal
½   teaspoon cayenne pepper
4   skinned trout fillets (about 1½ pounds
    total)
½   cup peanut oil

METHOD

PREPARATION: *For the Chili Hollandaise,* mince the onion, garlic, and bell peppers. In a small saucepan, heat the tablespoon of butter. Add the onion, garlic, and bell peppers and cook over low heat until soft, about 1 to 2 minutes. Add the chili powder, ¼ teaspoon black pepper, cayenne, and oregano and continue sautéing over low heat for 1 to 2 more minutes. Add the wine to the pan and stir with a wooden spoon to deglaze the bottom of the pan. Add the stock and reduce gently to ⅓ cup over low heat, about 10 minutes.

For the trout, mix together the sour cream, buttermilk, hot red-pepper sauce, mustard, egg yolks, 1 teaspoon salt, and ½ teaspoon black pepper until smooth. In a separate bowl, mix together the flour, cornmeal, cayenne, 1 tablespoon salt, and 1 tablespoon black pepper.

Recipe may be completed to this point several hours ahead.

COOKING AND SERVING: Dip each of the trout fillets into the sour cream mixture and then coat evenly with the flour mixture.

Make the Hollandaise. Add the stock mixture to the sauce. Keep warm.

Heat the peanut oil in a large frying pan over medium heat. Fry the fillets, turning once, until golden brown, about 5 minutes total. Drain.

Serve the trout with warm Chili Hollandaise.

YIELD: 4 servings

Larry Forgione
Chef/owner
An American Place
New York, NY

Monkfish Hash with Orange Hollandaise

Good old hash and eggs gain sophistication from succulent monkfish and a delicious orange hollandaise in this innovative dish.

INGREDIENTS

3	boiling potatoes (about 1 pound)
1½	pounds trimmed monkfish
½	onion
2	cloves garlic
1	rib celery
½	red bell pepper
½	green bell pepper
¼	cup chopped parsley
1	teaspoon minced fresh thyme

Poached Eggs

3	tablespoons vinegar
4	eggs

Orange Hollandaise

2	oranges
1	lemon
2	teaspoons white-wine vinegar
	Hollandaise Sauce (page 82)
	Salt and pepper
2	tablespoons butter
2	tablespoons oil
	Salt and coarse black pepper
	Pinch nutmeg
⅛	teaspoon cayenne pepper

METHOD

PREPARATION: Put the potatoes in a saucepan with cold, salted water to cover, bring to a boil, and cook until just tender, about 20 minutes. Drain and cool. Peel the potatoes and cut into thin slices.

Cut the monkfish into ¾-inch cubes. Mince the onion, garlic, and celery. Cut the bell peppers into ½-inch dice. Chop the parsley. Mince the thyme.

For the Poached Eggs, fill a saucepan ⅔ full with water, add the vinegar, and bring to a full boil. Break each egg into a cup or small bowl. Slide the eggs into the water 1 at a time. Turn the heat down to a bare simmer and poach the eggs until the white is just set but the yolk is still soft, about 3 minutes. Transfer cooked eggs to a bowl of cold water.

For the Orange Hollandaise, remove zest from 1 of the oranges and the lemon in 2-inch strips. Squeeze 3 tablespoons juice from the orange. In a small saucepan, combine orange juice, orange and lemon zests, and vinegar and cook over high heat until reduced to 2 tablespoons, about 5 minutes. Remove from heat and strain into a small, nonreactive bowl.

In a small frying pan, melt 1 tablespoon of the butter and sauté the onion, garlic, celery, and bell peppers until tender, about 5 minutes. Remove from heat.

Recipe can be done to this point a few hours ahead.

COOKING AND SERVING: Grate the zest from the remaining orange. Bring a saucepan of water to a boil to reheat the eggs. Make the Hollandaise Sauce. Add orange reduction and season with salt and pepper. Keep warm.

Reheat the pepper mixture. Heat the oil in a large frying pan. Sauté the sliced potatoes over medium heat until crisp and golden brown, about 5 minutes.

In another frying pan, melt the remaining tablespoon of butter over medium heat. Add the monkfish, salt, black pepper, nutmeg, and cayenne pepper and sauté over medium-high heat until golden brown and cooked through, about 5 minutes. Put eggs into the pan of hot water just long enough to reheat, about 30 seconds.

Combine the potatoes, pepper mixture, and monkfish and carefully toss with the parsley and thyme. Season to taste with salt and pepper. Mound the mixture on plates. Top each serving with a poached egg and Orange Hollandaise. Garnish with orange zest.

YIELD: 4 servings

Bradley Ogden
Executive Chef
Compton Place
San Francisco, CA

Crisp Fried Smelt

These delicious morsels, batter-dipped and deep-fried, are especially tasty when served with homemade tartar sauce.

INGREDIENTS

Tartar Sauce

1 egg yolk
1 teaspoon Dijon mustard
½ teaspoon lemon juice
½ teaspoon anchovy paste
  Salt and pepper
1 cup olive oil
1 small onion
2 teaspoons capers
2 cornichons
1 tablespoon chopped parsley, tarragon, and/or chives, optional
2 tablespoons cornichon liquid

Rice-Flour Batter

1 cup rice flour
1 cup water
  Salt and pepper

  Oil for frying
1 pound smelt or other small fish
  Salt and pepper
  Lemon wedges for garnish

METHOD

PREPARATION: *For the Tartar Sauce,* whisk together egg yolk, mustard, lemon juice, anchovy paste, ¼ teaspoon salt, and ⅛ teaspoon pepper. Whisk in the oil drop by drop at first and then, when the sauce has thickened, in a thin stream. Grate the onion. Chop the capers, cornichons, and herbs and add to the sauce along with grated onion and 2 tablespoons liquid from the jar of cornichons. Add salt and pepper to taste.

Tartar Sauce can be made a day ahead.

For the Rice-Flour Batter, stir together rice flour, water, 2 teaspoons salt, and 1 teaspoon pepper. Consistency should be like that of yogurt or sour cream. Add more flour or water as necessary.

Recipe can be made to this point several hours ahead.

COOKING AND SERVING: Heat oil in a deep fryer or large frying pan to 375°F to 400°F. Dip smelt one at a time into batter and gently lower into oil. Fry until golden, about 1½ minutes. Remove and drain on paper towels. Season to taste with salt and pepper.

Serve with Tartar Sauce and lemon wedges.

YIELD: 4 servings

Steven Raichlen
Restaurant critic
Boston Magazine

RICHARD FELBER

Swordfish Picatta

Succulent swordfish steaks take on a new look when sliced into thin medallions, quickly sautéed, and topped with lemon butter.

FOR THE FRESHEST FISH

Smell is the best indicator. Really fresh fish should have no odor or only a very delicate, almost sweet smell. Whole fish should have clear eyes, neither milky nor sunken, and fish steaks and fillets should be bright and shiny.

Make the fish store your last stop so fish goes unrefrigerated for the shortest amount of time possible. Fish love the cold—either put it directly on a tray of ice or bury it in the ice. Use it as soon as possible.

Steven Raichlen
Restaurant critic
Boston Magazine

INGREDIENTS

    2   lemons
    2   ounces Parmesan cheese (about ½ cup grated)
    3   eggs
    3   tablespoons flour, + more for coating fish
    ¼   cup milk
    1½ pounds swordfish
        Salt and pepper
    3   tablespoons butter
    3   tablespoons oil
  2 to 3 tablespoons capers

METHOD

PREPARATION: Cut the ends off one of the lemons and pare away the rind and all the white pith down to the flesh. Cut lemon into paper-thin rounds, removing any seeds.

Grate the cheese. Whisk the eggs. Whisk in the cheese, 3 tablespoons flour, and enough milk to make the batter the consistency of heavy cream.

Cut the fish across the grain into ¼-inch slices. Sprinkle with salt and pepper.

Recipe can be completed to this point several hours ahead.

COOKING AND SERVING: Heat the butter and oil in a large frying pan over medium heat. Dust the fish pieces with flour and dip them in the batter. Panfry them in the butter, turning once, until the coating is golden brown and the fish just tests done, about 3 minutes total. Transfer the fish to warm plates. Make a lemon butter sauce by squeezing the juice from the second lemon into the frying pan and stirring with a wooden spoon to deglaze the pan. Add salt and pepper to taste.

Top each piece of fish with a few capers and lemon slices. Pour lemon butter sauce over all.

YIELD: 4 servings

Grilled Salmon with Tarragon Sauce

RICHARD FELBER

Grilled salmon truly melts in your mouth when served with this heady tarragon sauce. Throw a handful of woodchips on the grill, such as cherry or apple, to give the salmon a delicate smoked flavor.

INGREDIENTS

1 tablespoon minced fresh tarragon *or* 1 teaspoon dried tarragon
4 salmon fillets (about 1½ pounds total)
2 tablespoons olive oil
Salt and pepper

Tarragon Sauce
2 tablespoons minced fresh tarragon *or* 2 teaspoons dried tarragon
1 shallot
1 cup dry white wine
1 cup fish stock or clam juice
½ cup heavy cream
Salt and pepper
4 tablespoons butter

Fresh tarragon leaves for garnish, optional

METHOD

PREPARATION: Mince 3 tablespoons fresh tarragon. Sprinkle the salmon with 1 tablespoon of the minced tarragon or 1 teaspoon dried tarragon, rub with oil, and marinate in the refrigerator for at least 1 hour.

For the sauce, mince the shallot. Put the wine, stock, shallot, and 1 tablespoon of the minced tarragon or 1 teaspoon dried tarragon in a nonreactive saucepan. Bring to a boil over medium-high heat and cook until reduced to approximately ¾ cup, about 10 minutes. Lower heat to medium, add heavy cream, and continue reducing until slightly thickened, about 5 minutes. Strain. Season to taste with salt and pepper.

Recipe can be done to this point several hours ahead.

COOKING AND SERVING: Heat the grill. Season salmon with salt and pepper. Grill both sides of the fillets until cooked through, about 8 minutes total. Reheat sauce. Over the lowest possible heat, whisk cold butter into the reduction, about a tablespoon at a time, adding another piece as each is almost incorporated. Butter should not melt completely but should soften to form a creamy sauce. Remove from heat and add the remaining tablespoon of tarragon, if using fresh. Surround salmon fillets with sauce and garnish with tarragon leaves.

YIELD: 4 servings

Tobie Nidetz
Chef
Carlucci Restaurant
Chicago, IL

Salmon Steaks with Corn and Sugar Snap Peas

Sweet corn and sugar snap peas complement salmon beautifully in this unique dish.

INGREDIENTS

- 2 shallots
- 1 small hot red pepper
- 6 ears corn *or* 3 cups frozen corn kernels
- ¼ pound sugar snap peas (about 1 cup)
- 1 scallion
- 1 tablespoon minced fresh chives
  Minced fresh parsley for garnish
- 4 salmon steaks (about 2 pounds total)
  Salt and pepper
- 4 tablespoons butter
- 2 tablespoons oil

METHOD

PREPARATION: Mince the shallots. Remove seeds and ribs from the hot red pepper and mince. Cut the corn from the cobs or thaw the frozen corn. Trim the sugar snap peas and the scallion. Cut the sugar snap peas and scallion on an angle into thin slices. Mince the chives and parsley.

Recipe can be prepared to this point several hours ahead.

COOKING AND SERVING: Season the salmon with salt and pepper. In a heavy frying pan, heat the butter and oil over medium-high heat. Add the salmon and sear for about 1 minute. Turn the salmon over, add the shallots and hot red pepper, and cook for 2 minutes more. Add ⅓ cup of water, cover, and cook for 3 minutes. Add the corn, cover, and cook for 3 minutes more. Test the salmon by gently pulling the flesh away from the center bone. It should just stick to the bone slightly. Gently stir in the peas, scallion, and chives. Season with salt and pepper to taste and heat through.

Put the salmon steaks on warm plates with the vegetables. Sprinkle with the parsley.

YIELD: 4 servings

Sheryl Julian
Food writer
The Boston Globe

Sautéed Tuna with Tomato Sauce

To dice an onion, *cut in half so it will lie flat, then cut into vertical slices alomst through to the root end.*

Holding the knife parallel to the counter, cut the slices into strips.

Cut the onion across the strips to produce dice.

Fresh tuna steak, always a treat, is especially good accompanied by this tomato sauce, redolent with red and green peppers.

INGREDIENTS

Tomato Sauce

1	**small onion**
1	**clove garlic**
1	**red bell pepper**
1	**green bell pepper**
4	**fresh tomatoes** *or* **1 cup canned tomatoes**
2	**ounces prosciutto or other ham**
1	**very small chili pepper** *or* **⅛ teaspoon cayenne pepper**
1	**teaspoon chopped fresh basil + more for garnish** *or* **½ teaspoon dried basil**
1	**teaspoon chopped fresh oregano** *or* **½ teaspoon dried oregano**
3 to 4	**tablespoons olive oil**
	Salt and pepper
⅛	**teaspoon cayenne pepper**

Sautéed Tuna

1	**large clove garlic**
4	**½- to ¾-inch-thick tuna steaks (about 1½ pounds total)**
2	**tablespoons olive oil**
	Salt and pepper

METHOD

PREPARATION: *For the Tomato Sauce,* dice the onion. Mince the garlic. Roast red and green peppers over a gas flame or charcoal grill or under broiler until the skin is charred. Rub off skin and remove seeds and ribs. Cut bell peppers into 1-inch pieces. Peel, seed, and chop the tomatoes. Cut ham into ¼-inch dice. Seed and mince the chili pepper. If using fresh herbs, chop the basil and oregano.

Heat the olive oil in a saucepan. Add the onion, garlic, bell peppers, chili pepper, and ham and sauté over medium heat until onion is soft, about 3 minutes. Add the tomatoes and herbs and increase the heat to high. Cook until most of the liquid has evaporated, about 3 minutes. Season with salt and pepper and cayenne to taste. Sauce should be highly seasoned.

Tomato sauce can be prepared a few days ahead.

For the sautéed tuna, cut the garlic into slivers. Using the tip of a paring knife, make tiny slits in the steaks and insert the slivers of garlic.

Recipe can be prepared to this point several hours ahead.

COOKING AND SERVING: Heat the tomato sauce. Heat the olive oil in a frying pan over medium-high heat. Season the fish steaks with salt and pepper and cook the steaks in the frying pan, turning once, until browned on each side and fish just tests done, about 6 minutes total.

Serve the tuna surrounded with tomato sauce. Sprinkle with chopped fresh basil if desired.

YIELD: 4 servings

Steven Raichlen
Restaurant critic
Boston Magazine

RICHARD FELBER

Hollandaise Sauce

*For the hollandaise,
whisk the egg yolks
vigorously until light-
colored and thick.*

*Slowly whisk the
melted butter into the
beaten yolks in a thin
stream.*

INGREDIENTS

6   ounces butter
3   egg yolks
2   tablespoons water
    Salt and pepper
2   teaspoons lemon juice, approximately

METHOD

COOKING: Melt the butter. In a small, heavy saucepan set over the lowest possible heat, whisk the egg yolks with the water, ½ teaspoon salt, and ¼ teaspoon pepper. Whisk constantly until the mixture is light and creamy. Remove from heat and gradually whisk in the warm butter in a thin stream. Squeeze in lemon juice to taste and salt and pepper if needed. To keep the sauce for a short time, set the pan in a larger pan half filled with warm water.

YIELD: 1 cup

MAKING HOLLANDAISE

As with beurre blanc, hollandaise depends on the emulsification of butter for its creamy consistency. However, egg yolks make emulsification less tricky. The biggest danger in making hollandaise is overheating, which can cook the yolks and cause the sauce to separate. This sauce is best served immediately, but you can keep it warm for a short period of time by keeping it in a tepid water bath or a wide-mouthed, insulated thermos and whisking periodically.

POULTRY

Roasted Chicken with Vegetables

RICHARD FELBER

When cooked to perfection, there is nothing finer than a simple roast chicken. Vegetables, cooked alongside the chicken, put delicious pan juices to good use.

ROASTING A CHICKEN TO PERFECTION

The difficulty in roasting chicken is that the white meat often dries out before the leg meat is sufficiently cooked. One school of thought suggests roasting the chicken breast-side down, but while the meat stays moist, the skin remains pale and flabby. A better solution is to put butter between the skin and the flesh prior to roasting. Gently loosen the breast skin without tearing by slowly working fingertips underneath from the neck end. Then spread the butter over breast flesh with a small spatula or fingers and pat the skin down again.

Pamela Parseghian
Food editor
COOK'S Magazine

INGREDIENTS

2   carrots
4   cloves garlic
2   small onions
2   ribs celery
1   4-pound roasting chicken
    Oil for rubbing chicken
    Salt and pepper

METHOD

PREPARATION: Peel and cut each carrot into 4 chunks and blanch in boiling, salted water with the unpeeled garlic for 5 minutes. Cut the onions in half vertically. Remove strings from the celery and cut each rib into 4 pieces.

Recipe can be completed to this point up to a few hours ahead.

COOKING AND SERVING: Heat the oven to 350°F. Rub the chicken with oil and sprinkle with salt and pepper, inside and out. Put the vegetables and chicken in a roasting pan large enough to hold them in a single layer and sprinkle the vegetables with salt. Roast in preheated oven until meat thermometer reads 180°F, about 1 hour. To test without a thermometer, poke the inner thigh with a fork. The first juices should run clear, and the last drops should be slightly pink. Remove chicken when done. If the vegetables are not quite cooked, return to the oven for another few minutes. Degrease pan juices.

Carve chicken and pour juices over the chicken and vegetables before serving.

YIELD: 4 servings

Old-Fashioned Fried Chicken

RICHARD FELBER

The best fried chicken ever.

For the Old-Fashioned Fried Chicken, disjoint by cutting between thigh and body and through joint.

Cut down the center of the breastbone to halve the breast.

Cut through the joint between the wing and the body.

INGREDIENTS

1 **4-pound chicken**
1 **cup flour**
   Salt and coarse black pepper
   Oil for frying

METHOD

PREPARATION: Cut chicken into 8 pieces. Combine the flour with 1 tablespoon salt and 2 teaspoons pepper.

Recipe can be made to this point several hours ahead.

COOKING AND SERVING: Dip the chicken pieces in water and dredge in flour mixture. In a frying pan, heat about 1½ inches of oil over high heat to 375°F. Add the chicken. When the temperature returns to 375°F, lower heat to medium. Cook until golden brown on both sides and almost done, about 15 minutes. Raise heat to medium-high and finish browning, about 5 minutes more. Drain chicken and serve.

YIELD: 4 servings

Pamela Parseghian
Food editor
COOK'S Magazine

Smoky Tarragon Chicken

BARBECUING PARTICULARS

When grilled properly and served immediately, barbecued chicken is a true delicacy.

- *There is no need to baste. Chicken skin has enough fat to self-baste.*
- *Put dark meat on the grill 10 to 15 minutes before white meat so that it will all be done at the same time.*
- *Always use tongs to turn chicken since piercing with a fork allows juices to escape.*
- *If you want to use wood chips, try a fruitwood, such as cherry, apple, or peach, which imparts a nice accent without overpowering the chicken. A handful of chips provides plenty of smoke—just soak in water for 20 minutes, and throw on the grill when coals are gray.*

Miriam Ungerer
Free-lance writer
Sag Harbor, New York

RICHARD FELBER

Serve this juicy chicken hot off the grill and you'll be astonished at how good this simple standard can be.

INGREDIENTS

- 2 **3-pound chickens**
- 1 **lemon**
- ¼ **cup minced fresh tarragon**
- ¼ **cup minced fresh parsley**
- ½ **cup olive oil**
-    **Salt and pepper**

METHOD

PREPARATION: Cut chickens into quarters. Chop off the backbones and flatten the breasts by delivering a smart blow with the flat of a cleaver or by pressing firmly with the palm of your hand. Remove last joint from wings. Cut several slits in the chicken legs. Squeeze juice from lemon. Mince the tarragon and parsley together.

Mix together the lemon juice, olive oil, tarragon and parsley. Rub the mixture into the chicken. Cover and marinate.

Recipe can be made to this point several hours ahead.

COOKING: Heat the grill. Season chicken pieces with salt and pepper. Put the dark-meat chicken pieces on the grill about 6 inches from the coals and cook, turning with tongs every 5 minutes, about 25 minutes in all. After cooking dark meat for about 12 minutes, throw soaked wood chips onto the coals, add chicken breast pieces, cover the grill, and let the smoke permeate the meat for at least 5 minutes. Uncover grill and continue cooking until meat tests done, about 7 minutes more.

YIELD: 4 servings

Chicken Breasts with Tarragon Cream Sauce

*Crusty Italian bread, sautéed to golden perfection, and a sprinkling of tarragon
give new meaning to creamed chicken on toast.*

INGREDIENTS

2½ teaspoons chopped fresh tarragon +
    sprigs for garnish *or* ¾ teaspoon dried
    tarragon
3   tablespoons butter
4   slices Italian bread
1   plum tomato for garnish, optional
4   large boneless chicken breasts (about
    1⅓ pounds total)
½   small onion
1½ cups chicken stock (page 30)
¾   cup heavy cream
    Salt and pepper
2   teaspoons arrowroot

METHOD

PREPARATION: Chop the tarragon.

Heat 1½ tablespoons of the butter in a large frying pan over medium heat. Fry the bread, turning once, until golden on each side, about 5 minutes total. Add remaining 1½ tablespoons of butter when turning bread.

Peel, seed, and dice the tomato.

Recipe can be made to this point several hours ahead.

COOKING AND SERVING: In a frying pan with a lid, combine the chicken, onion, stock, and tarragon. Bring just to a simmer over low heat and cook, covered, until just cooked through, about 8 minutes total. Remove chicken from the pan.

Bring stock to a boil over high heat and reduce by ⅓, about 5 minutes. Add the cream and season to taste with salt and pepper. Remove and discard onion.

Dissolve the arrowroot in 1 tablespoon of cold water and gradually whisk into sauce.

Return chicken to the sauce to coat and just heat through. Put croutons on warm plates and top with chicken and sauce. Garnish with sprigs of tarragon and diced tomato.

YIELD: 4 servings

Pamela Parseghian
Food editor
COOK'S Magazine

Lemony Chicken and Rice Salad

*This zesty salad can be completed a day ahead,
making it ideal for casual summer entertaining.*

INGREDIENTS

1½	pounds boneless chicken, dark and/or white meat
3	onions
3	cloves garlic
¼	cup chopped parsley
2	lemons
½	cup olive oil
	Salt and pepper
1⅓	cups rice
2	cups chicken stock (page 30)
¾	teaspoon allspice
⅓	cup pine nuts, optional

METHOD

PREPARATION: Cut the chicken into bite-size pieces. Mince the onions and garlic. Chop the parsley. Grate zest from one of the lemons and squeeze both lemons to make ⅓ cup juice.

Heat 3 tablespoons of the oil in a large, wide pot. Sprinkle the chicken with salt and sear in the pot, in batches if necessary, over high heat until golden, about 5 minutes. Remove chicken.

Put the onions, garlic, and a pinch of salt in the same pot over medium heat and cook until onions are soft, about 3 minutes. Add the rice and stir to coat with oil. Add the stock and bring to a simmer. Season with salt and pepper and cook, covered, over low heat for 10 minutes. Stir in reserved chicken and cook, covered, until rice is tender, about 5 more minutes. Remove pot from the heat and let sit, covered, for 15 minutes. Transfer chicken and rice to a bowl and cool.

Add the parsley, lemon juice, allspice, and remaining 5 tablespoons oil to the rice and chicken. Season to taste with salt and pepper. Refrigerate if not serving immediately.

Heat the oven to 350°F. Spread the pine nuts in a shallow baking pan and toast, stirring frequently, until golden, about 5 minutes.

Salad can be made a day ahead.

SERVING: Bring salad back to room temperature. Just before serving, adjust seasoning, and toss lemon zest and pine nuts over salad.

YIELD: 4 servings

Pamela Parseghian
Food editor
COOK'S Magazine

Cinzano-Glazed Hens with Garlic

While this recipe may call for a great deal of garlic, keep in mind that it is strongest in its raw state. The longer garlic cooks, the more the flavor mellows.

INGREDIENTS

4	**Cornish game hens**
	Salt and pepper
20	**cloves garlic**
	Olive oil for tossing garlic
1½	**cups Cinzano, approximately**
8	**chives**

METHOD

PREPARATION: Put hens in a nonreactive roasting pan, sprinkle with salt, and put 1 whole unpeeled garlic clove into each cavity. Peel remaining garlic, toss with oil, season with salt, and add to roasting pan. Pour the Cinzano over the hens and sprinkle liberally with pepper. Chop chives and scatter over the hens. Marinate hens in the refrigerator for at least 1 hour, or even overnight, basting occasionally.

Recipe can be made to this point a day ahead.

COOKING AND SERVING: Heat oven to 400°F. Put hens with marinade in preheated oven and roast about 15 minutes. Reduce heat to 325°F and roast until juices run clear when the inside of a thigh is pierced with a fork, about 30 minutes more depending on size of hens. If the pan juices dry up midway through roasting, tip any juices out of the hens' cavities, or pour 1 or 2 tablespoons more Cinzano into the roasting pan.

Serve hens surrounded by several cloves of roasted garlic and topped with the pan juices.

YIELD: 4 servings

Kathy Gunst
Free-lance writer
South Berwick, ME

Chicken and Squab Stew

ABOUT STEW

- When browning meat or poultry for stew, dry it well first so it won't steam in its own moisture, and brown only a few pieces at a time, or the temperature of the browning fat will drop, which also causes the meat to steam instead of brown.
- Reduce stew to a gentle simmer after it first comes to a boil.
- The meat or poultry and vegetables should fit snugly in the pot, requiring a minimum of liquid, so that the sauce's flavor is concentrated.

Anise-flavored fennel gives this adaptation of a classic continental stew a distinctive, gutsy flavor.

For the Chicken and Squab Stew, remove the legs. Then cut squab breast away from bone, leaving wing attached to breast. Reserve carcass.

INGREDIENTS

- 1 3½-pound chicken
- 2 squabs
- 3 cups Chicken and Squab Stock, recipe follows
- ½ cup Tomato Sauce, recipe follows
- ¼ cup olive oil
- 1 small fennel bulb
- 1 red bell pepper
- 4 carrots
- 2 turnips
- 2 ribs celery
- 1 leek
- 1 large onion
- ¼ cup minced fresh basil *or* 1 tablespoon dried basil
- 3 large cloves garlic
- 1 tablespoon minced fresh rosemary *or* ½ teaspoon dried rosemary
  Salt and pepper

METHOD

PREPARATION: Cut chicken into 8 pieces. Skin and bone breasts and split each in half crosswise. Reserve all bones. Cut squabs into 4 pieces. Bone breasts. Reserve all bones. Pat the chicken and squabs dry with paper towels.

Make the Chicken and Squab Stock. Make the Tomato Sauce.

In a large frying pan, heat the olive oil and brown the chicken and squab pieces, being careful not to crowd the pan. Transfer to a plate and set aside.

Cut fennel and bell pepper into ¼-inch strips. Dice the carrots, turnips, celery, leek, and onion. Mince the basil, garlic, and rosemary.

Put half the vegetables into a large pot. Season with salt and pepper and combine with half the basil, garlic, and rosemary. Put the chicken and squab pieces, except the breasts, on top of the vegetables, along with any accumulated juice. Cover with the remaining vegetables and seasonings. Pour stock over all. Cover tightly and bring slowly to a boil. Lower heat and simmer until tender, 1 to 1½ hours. Remove the meat and vegetables and set aside; strain the liquid. Degrease the liquid and return to the pot. Bring to a boil and reduce to 2½ cups, about 10 minutes. Add the Tomato Sauce to the liquid, bring to a boil, and adjust seasonings.

Recipe can be made a day ahead.

COOKING AND SERVING: Bring sauce to a simmer. Add browned chicken and squab breasts and poach until just cooked through, 5 to 6 minutes. Add the remaining chicken pieces, squab, and vegetables to the sauce, heat through, and serve.

YIELD: 4 servings

For the Chicken and Squab Stock, roast in the chicken and squab carcasses and necks, carrots, celery, and onion in olive oil until well browned.

Tomato Sauce

INGREDIENTS

- ½ small onion
- 1 small clove garlic
- 2 tomatoes *or* 8 ounces canned plum tomatoes
- 1½ teaspoons olive oil
- ¼ teaspoon sugar
  Salt and pepper
- 1 tablespoon chopped fresh basil or parsley

METHOD

PREPARATION: Chop the onion. Mince the garlic. Chop the tomatoes, if using fresh, or drain and chop canned tomatoes.

Heat the olive oil in a large frying pan. Add the onion and cook until soft but not brown. Add the garlic, tomatoes, sugar, and salt and pepper to taste. Stir, cover, and cook, until the tomatoes are soft, about 30 minutes. Chop the basil and add to the sauce. Cook for another 5 minutes. Puree in a food processor. Adjust seasoning to taste.

Tomato Sauce can be made several days ahead.

YIELD: ½ cup

Chicken and Squab Stock

INGREDIENTS

- 1 carrot
- 1 rib celery
- 1 onion
- 1 tomato
- ¼ cup olive oil
  Bones, necks, and trimmings from chicken and squabs
- 1 bouquet garni of thyme, bay, and parsley leaves
- 1½ quarts water
  Salt and pepper

METHOD

PREPARATION: Quarter the carrot, celery, onion, and tomato.

Heat oven to 450°F. Pour the olive oil into a large roasting pan. Add the chicken and squab bones, necks, and trimmings and the carrot, celery, and onion. Roast in preheated oven, stirring occasionally, until the vegetables and bones are browned but not burned, 30 to 40 minutes.

Add the tomato, bouquet garni, water, 1 teaspoon salt, and pepper to taste. Lower heat to 400°F and continue cooking until the liquid is reduced by half. Strain the stock and press the bones and vegetables with the back of a spoon to extract all liquid. Degrease.

Stock can be made a day ahead.

YIELD: 3 cups

Lydie Marshall
Free-lance writer
New York, NY

Sauté of Chicken Thighs with Leeks and Mushrooms

Pungent leeks and woodsy wild mushrooms lend their intense flavors to chicken thighs, making this one-dish meal both hearty and sophisticated.

INGREDIENTS

2 small leeks
¼ pound fresh morels or other mushrooms
2 tablespoons butter
4 chicken thighs (about 1⅓ pounds total)
Salt and pepper
½ cup dry white wine
¼ cup chicken stock (page 30)
½ cup heavy cream
⅛ teaspoon grated nutmeg

METHOD

PREPARATION: Cut the leeks in quarters lengthwise just down to the root end and rinse thoroughly under cold water, fanning the layers. Cut the leeks into julienne. Rinse the morels. Trim the tough stems from the morels and halve any very large ones.

Recipe can be prepared to this point several hours ahead.

COOKING AND SERVING: In a large frying pan, melt the butter. Sprinkle the chicken with salt and pepper. Sauté the chicken, skin side down, over medium heat until golden, about 4 minutes. Turn and sauté about 2 minutes more. Add the leeks and cook about 3 minutes. Add the wine and stock and bring to a simmer. Cover the pan and simmer gently, turning the chicken once, until done, 10 to 12 minutes. Remove the chicken to serving plates and keep warm.

Reduce the pan juices over high heat until slightly thickened, about 1 minute. Add the morels, lower the heat, and stir in the cream. Simmer gently until the sauce coats the back of a spoon, 2 to 3 minutes. Season lightly with nutmeg and salt and pepper. Pour over the chicken.

YIELD: 4 servings

Melanie Barnard
Free-lance writer
New Canaan, CT

Cornish Game Hens and Peaches
with Orange Curry Butter

*The Orange Curry Butter adds a wonderful sweet-sour flavor
to succulent hens and summer peaches.*

INGREDIENTS

Orange Curry Butter

- 2 lemons
- 2 large oranges
- 1 shallot
- 1 small clove garlic
- 5 ounces softened butter
- 1½ tablespoons curry powder or to taste
- ¼ cup unsweetened orange-juice concentrate
  Salt and pepper

- 4 Cornish game hens
- 2 tablespoons softened butter
- 2 large, firm peaches

METHOD

PREPARATION: *For the Orange Curry Butter,* grate 1½ teaspoons zest from lemon. Squeeze 3 tablespoons lemon juice. Grate 1½ tablespoons zest from the oranges. Chop the shallot. Mince the garlic. In a food processor, combine lemon and orange zests, shallot, garlic, butter, and curry powder and process until well blended. With the machine running, gradually add the lemon juice and orange-juice concentrate. Season to taste.

Butter can be made several days ahead. Cover and refrigerate. Return to room temperature when ready to use.

Put the hens, breast side up, on a work surface. Gently loosen the breast skin from the flesh starting at the neck end, being careful not to tear the skin. With your fingers or a small spatula, spread 2 tablespoons of the seasoned butter on the breast under the skin and pat the skin back in place. Reserve the remaining seasoned butter at room temperature. Spread ½ tablespoon of unseasoned butter over the skin of each hen.

Recipe can be made to this point an hour ahead.

COOKING AND SERVING: Heat oven to 450°F. Put hens on a rack in a roasting pan and put into preheated oven. Immediately turn heat down to 350°F and roast until cooked through and internal temperature reaches 180°F, about 45 minutes.

Halve and pit the peaches but do not peel them. Put the peaches cut side up in a shallow, ovenproof pan. Spread the reserved seasoned butter over the cut flesh. Add a little water to the bottom of the pan to keep peaches from scorching and put in oven 15 minutes before hens are done. Let hens rest for a few minutes. Serve each hen with a peach half on the side.

YIELD: 4 servings

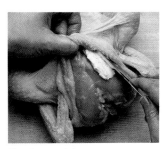

For the cornish game hens, spread Orange Curry Butter on the breast under the skin with fingers or a small spatula.

Elizabeth Riely
Free-lance writer
Newton Centre, MA

VINCENT LEE

Roast Turkey and Garbanzo-Chorizo Stuffing with Salsa Verde

The piquant flavors of the Southwest are a nice foil for the mild taste of turkey.

REMOVING THE WISHBONE

Removing a bird's wishbone before stuffing its neck cavity will make the cavity a bit roomier, as well as make carving a good deal easier. Lift the flap of neck skin and fold back. Cut down both sides of the wishbone. Pull the bone toward you and cut behind it to free it from the flesh.

Jane Butel
Free-lance writer
New York, NY

INGREDIENTS

Garbanzo-Chorizo Stuffing
Garbanzo beans, recipe follows, *or* 15 ounces canned garbanzo beans
1½ pounds chorizo
2 onions
2 large cloves Mexican garlic or 3 cloves regular garlic
1 pound chicken livers + liver from the turkey
2 tablespoons minced parsley
Salt
¼ pound butter

Salsa Verde
1 pound tomatillos *or* 13 ounces canned tomatillos
4 fresh, mild green chilies *or* 8 ounces canned chilies
½ onion
1 clove Mexican garlic or 1 large clove regular garlic
1 cup coriander leaves

1 15- to 17-pound turkey
1 tablespoon salt
¼ pound butter

METHOD

PREPARATION: *For the stuffing,* prepare garbanzo beans. If using canned, drain garbanzo beans. Remove casings from the chorizo and cut sausage into thin slices. Chop the onions. Mince the garlic. Trim and quarter the livers. Mince the parsley.

Cook chorizo in a large frying pan over medium-high heat until sausage is lightly browned. Drain all but 2 tablespoons of fat and add the garbanzo beans. Season with salt and cook until browned, about 15 minutes. Remove from heat.

In another frying pan, melt the ¼ pound butter. Add onions and garlic and cook until onions are soft. Add livers and fry, stirring until livers are crisp brown on the outside. Break up livers by mashing with a fork or potato masher. Combine with garbanzo beans and chorizo. Add parsley and salt to taste. Chill stuffing.

Stuffing can be made a day ahead.

For the Salsa Verde, remove husks and stems from tomatillos, if using fresh, and steam them until soft, about 5 minutes. Peel and seed chilies if using fresh. Or drain canned tomatillos and chilies. Chop the onion. Combine all ingredients in a food

VINCENT LEE

processor or blender until smooth. Allow sauce to sit at least an hour before serving to let flavors meld.

Salsa Verde can be made a few hours ahead.

COOKING AND SERVING: Heat oven to 400°F. Rub turkey inside and out with salt. Stuff neck and internal cavities of turkey with chilled stuffing. Truss. Put on a rack in a roasting pan and put into preheated oven. Melt the ¼ pound butter. Brush the turkey with butter every 15 minutes until juices collect and then continue to baste frequently with juices. Roast until turkey is golden brown and internal temperature of meat is 180°F at the meatiest part of the thigh, 3½ to 4 hours. Remove from oven and let rest for about 25 minutes before carving.

YIELD: 12 servings

Garbanzo Beans

INGREDIENTS

10 ounces dried garbanzo beans (1½ cups)
 1 rib celery
 1 onion
 1 carrot
 ¼ pound ham end or 1 pork bone or 3
     slices bacon
 1 bay leaf
 1 sprig thyme *or* ½ teaspoon dried thyme
 5 parsley stems
     Salt

METHOD

PREPARATION: Pick through beans and rinse with cold water. Put in a pan and add water to cover by 2 inches. Either soak for 8 to 10 hours or bring to a boil, cover, remove from heat, and set aside for 1 hour. Drain and rinse. Quarter the celery, onion, and carrot. Tie all ingredients except garbanzo beans and salt in cheesecloth bag.

In a large pot, combine beans, cheesecloth bag, and water to cover well. Bring to a boil, lower heat, and simmer, skimming occasionally, for an hour. Add salt and continue cooking until beans are tender, about ½ hour longer. Drain garbanzo beans and discard bag. Adjust seasoning.

Garbanzos can be made a few days ahead.

YIELD: 4 cups

Roast Capon with Cornbread, Bacon, and Pecan Stuffing

RICHARD FELBER

The stuffing for this capon is made with old-fashioned southern cornbread, but the gravy is a thoroughly modern sherry-based reduction sauce.

INGREDIENTS

Cornbread, Bacon, and Pecan Stuffing
⅓ cup Capon Stock, recipe follows *or* chicken stock (page 30)
1 loaf cornbread (about 2 cups crumbled), recipe follows
1½ ounces pecans (about ⅓ cup chopped)
1 rib celery
1 onion
1 capon liver, optional
¼ pound bacon
2 tablespoons butter
½ teaspoon dried thyme
½ teaspoon dried sage
Salt and pepper
¼ cup heavy cream
2 tablespoons dry sherry

1 tablespoon butter
1 7- to 8-pound capon
Salt and pepper

Sherry Cream Sauce
¾ cup dry sherry or white wine
1½ cups Capon Stock, recipe follows *or* chicken stock (page 30)
1½ cups heavy cream
Salt and pepper

METHOD

PREPARATION: Make the stock. You'll need about 2 cups in all. Make the cornbread and crumble 2 cups for the stuffing. Chop the pecans, celery, and onion. Mince the liver, if using.

Heat oven to 350°F. On a baking sheet, toast prepared cornbread and pecans in preheated oven until golden, about 10 minutes. In a large frying pan,

cook bacon until crisp. Drain, chop, and put in a large bowl. Pour off all but 2 tablespoons bacon drippings. Add cornbread and pecans to bacon.

Melt butter in the frying pan with bacon drippings. Add celery and onion and cook over medium heat, stirring frequently, until vegetables are tender, about 2 minutes. Stir in optional liver, thyme, sage, and salt and pepper to taste. Add to cornbread mixture.

Add cream, ⅓ cup stock, and the sherry to frying pan, stirring with a wooden spoon to deglaze the pan. Add to cornbread mixture and season to taste. Chill until ready to use.

Stuffing can be completed a day ahead.

COOKING AND SERVING: Heat oven to 400°F. Melt 1 tablespoon of butter for brushing capon. Season cavity of capon with salt and pepper. Stuff with cornbread mixture and truss. Brush with butter and sprinkle with salt and pepper. Roast capon in preheated oven for 15 minutes and then reduce heat to 350°F. Roast until juices run clear when the inner thigh is pierced and internal temperature of the meaty part of thigh reads 180°F, a total of 2½ to 3 hours. Transfer capon to a warm platter and let rest.

For the sauce, add sherry to roasting pan and bring to a boil, stirring with a wooden spoon to deglaze the pan. Add 1½ cups stock and any juices from resting capon and continue to boil, stirring often. Add cream and continue to boil until sauce is reduced to about 1¾ cups. Season sauce with salt and pepper and strain.

Remove stuffing, carve the capon, and pass Sherry Cream Sauce separately.

YIELD: 8 servings

Beverly Cox
Free-lance writer
Norwalk, CT

Capon Stock

INGREDIENTS

- 1 carrot
- 1 rib celery
- 1 small onion
- 1 clove
-   Neck and giblets (except liver) from capon, above
- 1 quart water
- ½ teaspoon salt
- ⅛ teaspoon black peppercorns

METHOD

PREPARATION: Cut the carrot and celery into 2-inch lengths. Halve onion and stick with the clove.

Put all ingredients into a large saucepan. Bring to a boil, skim, and then reduce heat. Simmer, uncovered, until liquid is reduced to approximately 2 cups, about 20 minutes. Strain, cool, and refrigerate stock until ready to use.

Stock can be made a couple of days ahead.

YIELD: about 2 cups

Cornbread

INGREDIENTS

- 1 egg
- 3 tablespoons butter
- 1 cup cornmeal
- ½ cup flour
- 1 cup milk
- 1 tablespoon baking powder
- ½ teaspoon salt

METHOD

PREPARATION: Heat oven to 400°F. Beat the egg. Melt the butter. Put an 8-inch ovenproof frying pan or baking pan in the oven. In a large mixing bowl, combine cornmeal, flour, milk, egg, 1 tablespoon of the butter, baking powder, and salt. Beat until smooth.

Melt remaining 2 tablespoons butter in heated pan and brush butter up sides of pan. Pour in batter. Bake on center rack in preheated oven until set and lightly browned, 25 to 30 minutes. Turn cornbread out onto a rack.

YIELD: 1 loaf

*1. **To truss a bird**, take a piece of kitchen twine and put the middle of it around the neck end of the bird. Wrap it under the drumsticks.*

2. Pull the string under the tail and cross it to hold the tail in a tucked-up position.

3. Wrap the string around the ends of the drumsticks to pull them close to the body.

4. Pull the drumsticks close to the bird and take the strings between the breast and drumsticks. Pull string together at neck and tie securely.

Pan-Roasted Quail

Tiny quail make an impressive meal easily.

INGREDIENTS

1	cup chicken stock (page 30)
12	quail livers or 4 chicken livers
6	tablespoons softened butter
12	quail
	Salt and pepper
2	teaspoons oil

METHOD

PREPARATION: Reduce chicken stock by ½ over medium-high heat, about 20 to 30 minutes. Puree the livers with 5 tablespoons of the butter in a food processor or blender and chill.

Season quail lightly with salt and pepper. Melt remaining tablespoon of butter, mix with oil, and coat the quail with a thin layer of butter and oil.

Recipe can be made to this point several hours ahead.

COOKING AND SERVING: Heat oven to 400°F. Cook the quail in ovenproof pans over medium-high heat until all sides are browned, about 5 minutes. Do not overcrowd pans. Put quail in preheated oven and roast until just done, about 5 to 7 minutes. Transfer quail to a warm serving platter and keep warm.

Degrease pan juices. Put roasting pan over medium-high heat and add reduced stock, stirring with a wooden spoon to deglaze. Lower heat to medium-low and whisk in chilled liver butter, a bit at a time. Cook until liver turns from pink to light brown, about 3 minutes. Adjust seasoning, strain, and serve along with quail.

YIELD: 4 servings

Brad Cole
Chef
Allegro on Boylston
Boston, MA

Mustard-Crumbed Duck Legs

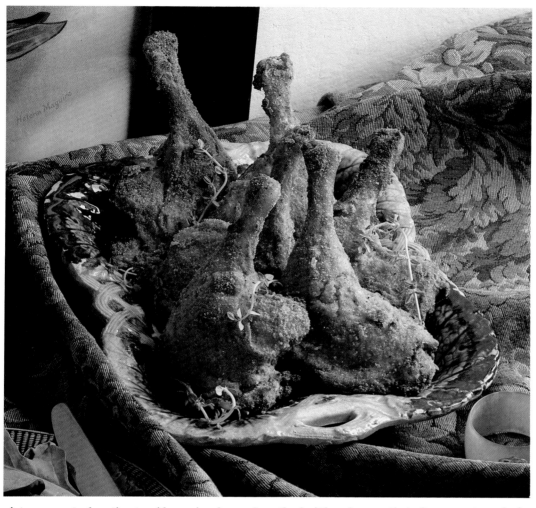

VINCENT LEE

A tangy mustard coating provides a nice change from the fruit-based sauces that often accompany duck.

INGREDIENTS

10	cups chicken stock (page 30)
4	duck legs (drumstick and thigh)
¼	cup Dijon mustard
¼	cup grainy mustard
½	cup fine bread crumbs
4	tablespoons butter

METHOD

PREPARATION: Bring stock to a simmer over low heat and add duck legs. Cook until tender, about 1 hour.

Recipe can be completed to this point several hours ahead.

COOKING AND SERVING: Heat oven to 400°F. In a small bowl, combine mustards. Remove duck legs from stock and pat dry. Spoon mustard mixture generously over duck pieces. Roll duck legs in bread crumbs, pressing gently to coat evenly. Shake off excess. Melt the butter. Brush a shallow baking dish lightly with some of the butter. Put the coated duck legs in the prepared baking dish, skin side up, and drizzle with some of the butter. Bake, basting occasionally with melted butter once legs begin to brown, until golden brown, 30 to 35 minutes. Serve hot.

YIELD: 4 servings

Richard Sax
Free-lance writer
New York, NY

Roast Goose Stuffed with Apples and Potatoes

A golden goose is dressed to perfection for the holidays.

GETTING YOUR GOOSE

Geese are gaining popularity in the U.S. and are now available in butcher shops and even some supermarkets. Since goose has a lot of bone per meat, allow about 1½ pounds per person.

INGREDIENTS

Stuffing

- ½ red onion
- ½ rib celery
- ¼ cup minced parsley
- 1 teaspoon minced fresh rosemary or ¼ teaspoon dried rosemary
- 1 teaspoon minced fresh chives *or* green onion tops
- 8 small boiling potatoes
- 2 apples
- 2 teaspoons oil
  Salt and pepper

- 1 9- to 10- pound goose
  Salt and pepper
- 1½ cups chicken stock (page 30)
- ⅛ cup arrowroot

METHOD

PREPARATION: *For the stuffing,* quarter the onion, cut crosswise into thin slices, and separate. Mince the celery, parsley, rosemary, and chives.

Remove necks, bones, and wing tips from the goose and reserve. Clean cavities of goose.

Recipe can be made to this point several hours ahead.

COOKING AND SERVING: Heat oven to 450°F. Bring a pot of salted water to a boil. Peel the potatoes and cut into ½-inch dice. Core and peel the apples and cut them into eighths. Put potatoes and apples into boiling water, return to a boil, and cook 2 minutes. Drain.

In a large, heavy pan, heat the oil. Add the onion and celery and sauté over medium heat until onion wilts, about 5 minutes. Add half the parsley, rosemary, and chives to the pan, reserving the other half. Mix in apples and potatoes, season with salt and pepper, and cool.

Season cavities of goose with salt. Stuff the bird and truss. Put neck bones and wing tips of goose in a large roasting pan. Put goose on top of bones. Roast for 20 minutes in preheated oven. Lower heat to 350°F. Add ¾ cup water to pan. Cover goose loosely with foil. Roast until meat thermometer reads 180°F or juices run clear when inside of leg is pierced, about 20 minutes per pound. Remove from pan and let goose rest ½ hour.

Meanwhile, for the sauce, remove as much fat as possible from the pan. Add chicken stock and simmer for about 5 minutes, scraping the bottom of the pan with a wooden spoon to deglaze. Remove bones from pan and strain stock into a saucepan. Bring to a simmer.

Dissolve arrowroot in ⅛ cup water. Slowly pour half of this mixture into sauce, whisking constantly. Season to taste with salt and pepper. Add more arrowroot mixture until sauce is the desired thickness.

Remove stuffing from goose and toss with remaining herbs. Carve the bird and pass the sauce separately.

YIELD: 6 servings

Pamela Parseghian
Food editor
COOK'S Magazine

MEAT

Veal Rib Roast with Cream Sauce

Thyme Crêpes with Chanterelles and Veal

Veal Sausage with Greens

Pork Tenderloin with Summer Apples and Plums

Pork, Leek, and Potato Stir-Fry

Prune-Stuffed Pork with Onion Gravy

Not-Like-Mom's Meatloaf

American Breakfast Sausage

Beef Tenderloin with Thyme and Shallot Butter

Tenderloin au Poivre

Mustard-Roasted Rack of Lamb

Grilled Lamb on Cabbage Leaves

Lamb Chili with Jalapeno Hominy

Veal Rib Roast with Cream Sauce

A simple cream sauce laced with garlic accents this delectable, luxurious roast perfectly.

FOR EASIER CARVING

To make it easier for you to slice the veal roast into four portions, ask your butcher to cut just through the chine bone (the bone to which the ribs connect) or remove the chine bone entirely. Have the butcher reserve the bones and trimmings for you since they make an ideal "rack" on which to place your roast in the pan. They'll keep the roast above the drippings while making the drippings especially flavorful.

INGREDIENTS

Cream Sauce
1 clove garlic
1 cup chicken stock (page 30) or veal stock
½ cup heavy cream
 Salt and pepper

1 rack of veal (about 3½ pounds)
 Salt and pepper

METHOD

PREPARATION: Mince the garlic.
 This can be done several hours ahead.

COOKING AND SERVING: Heat oven and a roasting pan to 500°F. Season the entire roast generously with salt and pepper. Put roast in the roasting pan and sear in preheated oven for 15 minutes. Lower heat to 350°F and roast until internal temperature is 130°F for a pink roast, approximately 40 minutes (about 16 minutes per pound). Let roast rest for about 20 minutes.
 For the sauce, degrease the pan juices, add the garlic, and cook over medium heat until soft, about 30 seconds. Add the stock to drippings, stirring with a wooden spoon to deglaze. Cook over medium-high heat until reduced and syrupy, about 5 minutes. Add heavy cream and cook for 2 minutes more. Season with salt and pepper to taste. Strain sauce.
 Remove strings from the roast and cut meat, against the grain and at a slight angle, into thick or thin slices as desired. Serve sauce on the side.

YIELD: 4 servings

Pamela Parseghian
Food editor
COOK'S Magazine

Thyme Crêpes with Chanterelles and Veal

RICHARD FELBER

*These crêpes combine classic French luxuries—
veal, wild mushrooms, and truffles—for a dish
that is truly special. The truffles are optional.*

INGREDIENTS

Thyme Crêpes
1 teaspoon fresh thyme *or* ¼ teaspoon
  dried thyme
1 teaspoon butter
1 egg
  Salt and pepper
¾ cup milk + more, if necessary
½ cup flour

½ pound fresh chanterelles or other
  mushrooms
2 shallots
1 pound veal shoulder
3 scallions
6 tablespoons butter
  Salt and pepper
½ cup white wine
2½ cups chicken stock (page 30)
2 tablespoons flour
½ cup heavy cream
¼ cup black truffles, optional

METHOD

PREPARATION: *For the Thyme Crêpes,* remove the
leaves from the thyme stems. Melt 1 teaspoon butter. Whisk together the egg, ¼ teaspoon salt and
⅛ teaspoon pepper, the teaspoon butter, and ¾ cup
milk. Add flour slowly, whisking continuously. Add
thyme leaves. Let batter rest for about 20 minutes.
Add more milk, if necessary, to make batter the
consistency of heavy cream.

Heat a 6-inch crêpe pan or small, nonstick frying pan over medium heat. Lightly butter the pan
if necessary. Pour about 3 tablespoons batter into
the pan, tilting the pan so that the batter covers the
bottom evenly. Cook until the edges look slightly
dry, about 1 minute, turn, and cook until just golden,
about 30 seconds more. Repeat with remaining batter. Stack with plastic wrap or waxed paper between
crêpes. Wrap well if not using immediately.

Crêpes can be completed a few days ahead, or
they can be frozen.

Separate mushroom stems from caps. Halve or
quarter the caps, depending on size. Trim the stems
and cut diagonally into ¼-inch slices. Mince the
shallots. Cut the veal into ½-inch dice. Trim the
scallions and cut them diagonally into ⅛-inch slices,
including some of the green.

Heat 2 tablespoons of the butter in a large frying
pan. Sauté the mushroom stems and caps until
heated through, about 1 minute. Remove mushrooms with a slotted spoon. Add 2 more tablespoons of the butter to the frying pan. Add the
shallots and sauté for 30 seconds. Season veal
lightly with salt and pepper, add it to the pan, and
cook over medium-high heat until well seared.

Add the wine to the frying pan, stirring with a
wooden spoon to deglaze. Add stock and simmer,
uncovered, stirring occasionally, until meat is
tender, about 40 minutes. Add any mushroom juices
that may have accumulated. If cooking liquid is
reduced by more than half, add water.

Melt the remaining 2 tablespoons of butter in a
small pot over medium-low heat. Add the flour and
stir constantly until just golden. Remove from heat
and whisk in cream. Add to veal, whisking until
smooth. Bring to a simmer and add sautéed
mushrooms. Cook over low heat, stirring frequently, for 10 more minutes. Season to taste.
Remove from heat. Remove and reserve about ½
cup of the mushrooms with some of the sauce.
Grate truffles into pan, add all but 1 tablespoon of
the scallions, and stir.

Butter a baking dish. Put ⅛ of the filling in the
center of each crêpe. Roll each crêpe and place
seam-side down in the prepared baking dish. Top
crêpes with reserved mushrooms and sauce.

Recipe can be completed several hours ahead.

COOKING AND SERVING: Heat oven to 350°F. Bake
crêpes in preheated oven until just heated through,
about 15 minutes.

Sprinkle crêpes with reserved scallions.

YIELD: 4 servings

Pamela Parseghian
Food editor
COOK'S Magazine

Veal Sausage with Greens

To stuff sausages, pull almost the whole length of casing over the neck of the stuffer, holding the end of the casing out straight so that it does not get twisted.

Send a bit of meat through to eliminate air from the feed tube and then knot the dangling end of casing.

Fill the casing until just taut. Let the filled sausage fall into a coil to minimize stress on casing.

Judy Rodgers
Chef
Berkeley, CA

NANCY McFARLAND

These grilled sausages are especially light, thanks to the addition of veal and greens.

INGREDIENTS

1	pound boneless lean veal leg
2	ounces "green" pork belly (uncured bacon) or pancetta
¼	pound boneless pork butt with about 30 percent fat content
4	ounces fatback
3	tablespoons heavy cream
3	tablespoons fresh bread crumbs
1	tablespoon grated Parmesan cheese, optional
	Pinch of ground nutmeg
	Salt
3	cups greens, such as arugula, chicory, or spinach
1½	teaspoons butter
1½	feet hog casing *or* ½ pound caul fat
1	large red onion
1	red bell pepper
¼	cup olive oil

METHOD

PREPARATION: Put the veal, pork belly, and pork butt through a meat grinder using a plate with ¼-inch holes. Cut the fatback into chunks and add to the ground meat. Chill the mixture and grind again.

Heat the cream and soak the bread crumbs in it. Grate the cheese. Combine the meat mixture with the soaked bread crumbs and cheese and season with nutmeg and about 1½ teaspoons salt.

Trim and wash the greens. Chop ½ cup of the greens. In a frying pan, melt the butter over medium heat and sauté the chopped greens until just wilted. Drain and chill.

Combine the chilled greens with the meat mixture. Fry a small patty of the mixture, taste, and adjust the seasoning. Stuff the remaining meat mixture into hog casing or shape loosely into 3- to 4-ounce patties and wrap each in a bit of caul fat.

Cut the onion and red pepper into thick slices.

Recipe can be made to this point several hours ahead.

COOKING AND SERVING: Heat the grill. Drizzle the olive oil over the onion and pepper slices and put them on the grill with the sausages. Turn vegetables and sausages once while cooking. Grill until sausages just lose their pink color, about 8 minutes.

Put the sausages on plates and garnish with the remaining greens and grilled onion and pepper slices.

YIELD: 4 servings

Pork Tenderloin with Summer Apples and Plums

Calvados and crème fraîche add lushness to this quick sauté.

INGREDIENTS

1⅓ **pounds pork tenderloin**
2   **shallots**
3   **plums**
    Minced fresh parsley for garnish
3   **apples**
½   **lemon**
2   **tablespoons butter**
2   **tablespoons oil**
    Salt and pepper
¾   **cup ruby port**
¼   **cup Calvados or other apple brandy**
½   **cup chicken stock (page 30)**
¼   **cup crème fraîche**

METHOD

PREPARATION: Cut the pork into ¼-inch-thick slices. Mince the shallots. Quarter and pit the plums. Mince the parsley.

Recipe can be made to this point several hours ahead.

COOKING AND SERVING: Peel and core the apples and cut them into ¼-inch-thick wedges. Squeeze the lemon juice over apples and toss.

In a heavy frying pan, heat the butter and oil over medium-high heat. Season pork slices with salt and pepper and lightly brown the pork on one side. Turn, scatter the shallots around the meat, and cook until shallots are soft, about 3 minutes. Add the port, Calvados, stock, plums, and apples. Lower the heat to medium, cover, and simmer just until the pork loses its pink color, about 5 minutes. Remove the meat and a few apple wedges for garnish and keep warm.

Puree the remaining fruit and cooking liquid. Return the puree to the pan and bring to a boil. Whisk in the crème fraîche. Season with salt and pepper to taste.

Coat 4 warm plates with the sauce. Arrange the pork on the sauce and garnish with the reserved apple wedges. Sprinkle with the parsley.

YIELD: 4 servings

Sheryl Julian
Food writer
The Boston Globe

Pork, Leek, and Potato Stir-Fry

RICHARD FELBER

East meets West in this innovative stir-fry that adds such exotic flavors as ginger and sesame oil to the traditional combination of pork and apple.

INGREDIENTS

       2 **tablespoons sesame seeds**
       1 **pound broccoli**
       1 **large carrot**
       1 **clove garlic**
       2 **teaspoons minced fresh ginger**
       1 **pound boneless pork tenderloin**
       2 **leeks**
       2 **teaspoons cornstarch**
       2 **tablespoons chicken stock (page 30)**
       2 **tablespoons soy sauce, plus more for seasoning**
       2 **small red potatoes**
       1 **large tart apple, such as Cortland or Granny Smith**
  2 to 3 **tablespoons peanut oil**
         Salt and pepper
       ½ **cup whole cashews**
         Few drops sesame oil, optional

METHOD

PREPARATION: Toast the sesame seeds in a 325°F oven until golden, 5 to 10 minutes. Peel the broccoli stems. Cut the stems into ⅛-inch-thick diagonal slices. Cut the tops into florets. Blanch the broccoli in boiling, salted water until just tender. Drain, plunge into cold water, and drain again.

Cut the carrot into ⅛-inch-thick diagonal slices. Mince the garlic and the ginger. Trim the pork of all sinew and cut it into ¼-inch-thick by 1½-inch- long strips. (Freezing the meat just before slicing makes cutting easier.) Trim the leeks, leaving about 3 inches of green, quarter lengthwise to just above the root end, and rinse under cold water, fanning the layers. Cut crosswise into ⅛-inch-thick slices.

Recipe can be made to this point several hours ahead.

COOKING AND SERVING: Dissolve the cornstarch in the stock and soy sauce. Cut the unpeeled potatoes into ⅛-inch by 1½-inch julienne strips and rinse them with cold water. Cut the unpeeled apple into eighths, core, and then cut crosswise into ⅛-inch-thick slices.

Heat 2 tablespoons of the peanut oil in a wok or very large frying pan over high heat. When very hot, add the carrot. Cook for 1 minute and then add the potatoes. Season with salt and pepper. Stir-fry until the potatoes start to turn golden, about 2 minutes. Stir in the garlic and ginger, add the pork strips and more oil if necessary, and stir-fry to sear, about 2 minutes. Add the leeks and stir-fry until they are bright green, about 30 seconds. Stir in the broccoli and make a well in the center of the wok. Stir the cornstarch mixture into the well. Add the sliced apple and cook until the liquid thickens. Add the cashews, sesame seeds, and sesame oil, and stir just to combine. Season with salt and pepper and soy sauce to taste.

YIELD: 4 servings

Pamela Parseghian
Food editor
COOK'S Magazine

Prune-Stuffed Pork with Onion Gravy

Succulent prunes are a traditional and delicious complement to pork.

INGREDIENTS

Prune Stuffing
1½ cups pitted prunes
5 slices white bread
1 small rib celery
1 small onion
1 small green bell pepper
   Salt and pepper
¾ cup chicken stock (page 30)

1 boneless pork loin (about 6 pounds)

Onion Gravy
½ onion
¼ cup chopped parsley
   Drippings from roast pork
6 tablespoons flour
3 cups chicken stock (page 30) or water
1 cup rosé wine
   Salt and pepper

METHOD

PREPARATION: *For the stuffing,* simmer prunes in ¾ cup water until plump and tender, about 10 minutes. Drain and chop. Cut bread into ½-inch cubes (you should have about 3 cups). Dice celery, onion, and bell pepper. In a bowl, combine prunes, bread cubes, celery, onion, bell pepper, ¾ teaspoon salt, and ¼ teaspoon black pepper. Moisten mix-ture with chicken stock.

Butterfly the pork loin by slicing in half almost all the way through horizontally. Pound pork to an even thickness, just under 1 inch. Spread stuffing over pork, roll up like a jelly roll from the long side, and tie with string at about 1½-inch intervals.

For the gravy, mince the ½ onion. Chop the parsley.

Recipe can be made to this point several hours ahead.

COOKING AND SERVING: Heat oven and a roasting pan to 500°F. Put pork in roasting pan and sear in preheated oven for 15 minutes. Lower heat to 350°F and roast pork until internal temperature reaches 140°F, about 25 more minutes. Transfer roast to a warm platter to rest for about 20 minutes.

For the gravy, measure ⅓ cup of the drippings and pour off remaining drippings. Heat the ⅓ cup drippings in roasting pan over medium heat. Add the onion and parsley and cook until the onion is soft, about 4 minutes. Add flour and cook, stirring oc-casionally, about 5 minutes. Add the stock and wine and cook, stirring occasionally, about 5 more minutes. Season to taste with salt and pepper.

Cut strings from roast and slice. Pass gravy separately.

YIELD: 12 servings

Richard Perry, owner
Gregg Mosberger, chef
Richard Perry Restaurant
St. Louis, MO

107

Not-Like-Mom's Meatloaf

This is a luxury meatloaf aromatic with herbs, wild mushrooms, and the finest Virginia-cured bacon. Leftover, chilled, and sliced thin, it can be served like a pâté.

INGREDIENTS

2	slices white bread
½	ounce dried morels, boletes, shiitake, or matsutake
2	large cloves garlic
1	onion
½	cup minced parsley
½	pound domestic mushrooms
3	tablespoons butter
1½	pounds lean ground chuck or ground flank steak
1	pound fatty ground pork shoulder
1	pound lean ground veal
¼	cup bourbon
	Salt and coarse black pepper
1	extra large egg
½	teaspoon dried thyme
4 to 5	thin strips Virginia-cured bacon

METHOD

PREPARATION: In a food processor, make fine crumbs from the bread. Soak dried mushrooms in enough warm water to cover. Mince the garlic, onion, and parsley. Chop the fresh mushrooms.

Melt butter in a saucepan, add garlic, onion, and fresh mushrooms and sauté until tender, about 4 minutes. Strain the mushroom-soaking liquid through a sieve lined with several layers of cheesecloth or a coffee filter into a pan. Chop the reconstituted mushrooms into fairly small pieces and cook in the strained soaking liquid over high heat until liquid is reduced to just a few tablespoons.

Recipe can be made to this point several hours ahead.

COOKING AND SERVING: Heat oven to 350°F. In a bowl, combine ground meats with bourbon and 1 tablespoon coarse pepper. Beat the egg and add to the meat mixture along with the bread crumbs, parsley, thyme, fresh and dried mushrooms, and 4 teaspoons salt. Blend well.

Pack meatloaf into a 2-quart loaf pan or into two 1-quart loaf pans. Lay bacon slices over the top. Cover with a double thickness of foil.

Set loaf pan(s) in a larger pan and pour boiling water to come halfway up the sides of the loaf pan(s). Bake in preheated oven until thermometer, poked through the foil and into center of the loaf, reads 170°F, about 1 hour and 15 minutes for large loaf, 45 minutes for the small loaves. Raise heat to 375°F, uncover, and cook until browned, about 15 more minutes.

Let loaf rest in its own juices for at least 30 minutes before removing from pan.

YIELD: 6 servings

Miriam Ungerer
Free-lance writer
Sag Harbor, NY

American Breakfast Sausage

These homemade sausages, juicy and redolent with sage, are so easy to prepare you may never tolerate store-bought sausages again.

NANCY McFARLAND

INGREDIENTS

1   **boneless pork butt with about 30 percent fat content (about 5 pounds)**
2   **large cloves garlic**
2   **tablespoons fresh sage *or* 2 teaspoons dried sage**
2   **teaspoons crushed dried hot red pepper or to taste**
     Salt and coarse black pepper
     Flour for coating sausage patties
     Butter for frying

METHOD

PREPARATION: Cut the pork into chunks and grind in a meat grinder, using a plate with ¼-inch holes. Chop the garlic. Chop the sage, if fresh.

In a bowl, combine the ground pork with the garlic, sage, hot red pepper, and about 4 teaspoons salt and 2 tablespoons pepper. Fry a small patty, taste, and adjust the seasoning if necessary. Refrigerate remaining mixture for at least 30 minutes.

Recipe can be made to this point a day ahead.

COOKING: Shape the mixture into small patties and flour lightly. Over medium heat, melt enough butter in a frying pan to film the bottom of the pan and fry the patties until they just lose their pink color, about 4 minutes per side.

YIELD: 4 servings

Judy Rodgers
Chef
Berkeley, CA

Beef Tenderloin with Thyme and Shallot Butter

For the Beef Tenderloin with Shallot Butter, cut off the chain or side strap, a fat-encased piece of meat running lengthwise along the roast.

To remove the silverskin, the tough membrane on top of the tenderloin, slide a knife just below it.

This cut is more tender but less flavorful than other cuts. Herbed butter adds both flavor and moisture.

INGREDIENTS

- 1 beef tenderloin (about 1¾ pounds, untrimmed)
- 1½ teaspoons minced fresh thyme *or* ½ teaspoon dried thyme
- 1 small shallot
- 4 tablespoons + 1 teaspoon softened butter
  Salt and pepper
  Oil for brushing beef

METHOD

PREPARATION: To insure uniform slices of beef, trim off the chain, or side strap, a long strip of meat encased in fat that runs along the side of the tenderloin, and save for a sauté. Trim the tenderloin of all fat and silverskin (the tough membrane beneath the fat). Reserve some trimmings. With a paring knife, make a central tunnel for the stuffing by putting it in from each end of the meat. Put a finger in each hole to make sure the tunnel meets in the middle.

Mince the thyme and shallot. In a small pot, melt about 1 teaspoon of the butter and sauté the thyme and shallot over low heat until shallot is soft, about

1 minute. Cool slightly. In a small bowl, combine the remaining 4 tablespoons butter, thyme-shallot mixture, and plenty of salt and pepper.

Recipe can be made to this point several hours ahead.

Put the flavored butter in a pastry bag fitted with a plain tip. Pipe the butter into the roast from each end. Or shape the butter into a thin cylinder, put in freezer to firm, and insert the cylinder into the tunnel. Plug the ends of the tunnel with reserved meat trimmings and tie the roast to secure ends.

Recipe can be completed several hours ahead.

COOKING AND SERVING: Heat oven and roasting pan to 500°F. Coat roast with oil and sprinkle with salt and pepper. Carefully put roast in pan and sear in preheated oven for 10 minutes. Lower heat to 350°F and roast until internal temperature is 125°F for medium-rare, about 12 minutes more. Let roast rest for about 20 minutes.

Remove string and carve the roast into thick or thin slices as desired, against the grain and at a slight angle. Serve any juices with the meat.

YIELD: 4 servings

Pamela Parseghian
Food editor
COOK'S Magazine

Tenderloin au Poivre

RICHARD FELBER

Nothing suitable for outdoor cookery could be simpler or more luxurious than this meltingly tender cut of beef grilled whole and then cut into succulent servings.

ABOUT TENDERLOINS

The old adage that states that meat cut "farthest from hoof and horn" is most tender is true, since this is where muscles are least exercised. The most tender cut of all is the tenderloin, a long, boneless, cylindrical muscle running along the back, where it has little work to do.

Beef tenderloin needs barding or constant basting or it will dry out. If you can't find the fresh, unsalted pork fat called for here, use a slab of salt pork cut into large, thin squares. Rinse the salt pork thoroughly under cold water and dry.

INGREDIENTS

1 beef tenderloin (about 1¾ pounds, untrimmed)
2 tablespoons combination of green, white, and black peppercorns
½ pound thin-sliced fresh pork fat
¼ pound butter
¼ cup cognac, optional
  Salt

METHOD

PREPARATION: Cut off the tenderloin's chain or sidestrap, a long strip of meat encased in fat that runs along the side, and reserve for another use, such as a stir-fry. Trim fat from beef.

Crush the peppercorns and rub into the meat.

Wrap the pork fat around the tenderloin and tie at 1½-inch intervals. Let rest at room temperature at least half an hour or refrigerate up to 3 hours. Return roast to room temperature before grilling.

COOKING AND SERVING: Heat the grill and let coals burn down to a steady glow. Melt the butter.

Grill the tenderloin, turning frequently, until internal temperature reaches 125°F for medium-rare, about 30 minutes. Let rest for about 20 minutes. Remove strings from the tenderloin. Cut into slices and pour melted butter over the top.

In a small pot, carefully heat the cognac, light it, and pour a little over the beef. Sprinkle with salt just before serving.

YIELD: 4 servings

Miriam Ungerer
Free-lance writer
Sag Harbor, NY

A SEARING DEBATE

Is it better to sear the meat at high heat first, or will a roast be juicier and more flavorful if cooked at one low temperature throughout? Searing is the way to go. Whether or not it actually seals in juices may be debatable, but searing will certainly produce as juicy a roast as cooking at one temperature, and nicely browned meat is definitely more flavorful and eye-pleasing than a pallid roast.

To sear, preheat oven to a hot temperature—usually 450°F to 500°F. Professional cooks find preheating the empty roasting pan aids in searing. Sear for 10 to 15 minutes, depending on the cut of meat, before reducing heat. Especially lean cuts, such as tenderloin, and roasts with a coating, such as the mustard-covered rack of lamb here, should be seared for only 10 minutes to prevent drying out or burning.

Pamela Parseghian
Food editor
COOK'S Magazine

Mustard-Roasted Rack of Lamb

A simple, robust coating of mustard and salt complements the full flavor of the rack of lamb.

INGREDIENTS

2 8-rib racks of lamb (about 1¾ pounds each)
¼ cup mustard
   Coarse salt

METHOD

PREPARATION: Trim fat from between bones and scrape the protruding bones clean with a paring knife. Trim excess fat from meat, leaving a thin layer.

Meat can be prepared several hours ahead.

COOKING AND SERVING: Heat the oven and a roasting pan to 450°F. Mix the mustard and 2 tablespoons of coarse salt in a small bowl. Coat the racks with the mixture. Put the coated racks in preheated roasting pan and sear in preheated oven for 10 minutes. Reduce heat to 350°F. Cover loosely with foil if either the coating or the bones are browning too quickly. Cook until internal temperature reaches 130°F for medium-rare, about 20 minutes more (approximately 17 minutes per pound). Let rest for about 20 minutes.

Slice between the bones to divide into portions.

YIELD: 4 servings

For the rack of lamb, carve by cutting between the ribs.

Grilled Lamb on Cabbage Leaves

Orange and coriander combine to create a zesty marinade for lamb, just barely grilled and served on a bed of grilled cabbage leaves. The dish can also be made in the broiler.

INGREDIENTS

Lamb Marinade
1 clove garlic
1 small onion
½ orange
1 teaspoon ground coriander
¼ cup olive oil
⅓ cup sherry or Madeira
    Salt and pepper

1 pound boneless leg of lamb
4 large leaves savoy cabbage or other green cabbage
2 cups chicken stock (page 30) or water
4 tablespoons butter
    Salt and pepper
½ teaspoon ground coriander
1½ teaspoons minced fresh thyme *or* ½ teaspoon dried thyme

METHOD

PREPARATION: *For the marinade,* chop the garlic. Slice the onion. Put garlic and onion in a nonreactive bowl large enough to hold the lamb and squeeze in the orange juice. Add the 1 teaspoon coriander, the oil, sherry, salt and pepper.

Cut the lamb into ¼-inch-thick slices. Put the meat in the marinade, turn to coat, cover with plastic wrap, and refrigerate for at least 5 hours, turning occasionally.

Recipe can be made to this point 3 days ahead.

Remove the tough ribs from cabbage leaves. In a saucepan, bring the stock to a simmer. Add the cabbage, cover, and cook over medium heat until the leaves are just tender, about 5 minutes. Remove the leaves carefully and let them cool. Reserve the cooking liquid for another dish, such as soup.

Recipe can be made to this point several hours ahead.

COOKING AND SERVING: Heat the grill. Melt the butter. Brush cabbage leaves on both sides with melted butter and season with salt and pepper. Remove the meat from the marinade and sprinkle it with ½ teaspoon coriander, thyme, and salt and pepper. Put the meat and butter-brushed cabbage leaves on the grill and cook until the meat is medium-rare and the cabbage leaves are lightly browned, about 2 minutes per side.

Put cabbage leaves on plates and top with meat.

YIELD: 4 servings

Pamela Parseghian
Food editor
COOK'S Magazine

Lamb Chili with Jalapeno Hominy

Mild hominy combines with hot jalapeno. Ground lamb adds a rich, distinctive flavor.

SPICING YOUR CHILI

When buying chili powder, pursue purity. Most store-bought chili powders are blends including salt, dried garlic, and other herbs and spices. We prefer to use a pure, mild chili powder and add fresh garlic and our own choice of other seasonings, as in this recipe. If you have a hard time finding the chili powder, use paprika.

INGREDIENTS

2	tablespoons cumin seeds *or* 1½ tablespoons ground cumin
2	small yellow onions
2	large cloves garlic
2	cups canned Italian plum tomatoes
3½	cups white or yellow hominy (about 30 ounces canned)
1½	pounds boneless shoulder of lamb *or* 1½ pounds coarse-ground lamb Salt and pepper
2	tablespoons olive oil
2½	tablespoons ground mild red chili
1	teaspoon allspice
½	teaspoon ground cinnamon
½	teaspoon dried thyme
½	teaspoon dry mustard
1 to 1½	tablespoons cornmeal, if necessary
1	jalapeno pepper
3	tablespoons butter

METHOD

PREPARATION: In a heavy skillet, toast the cumin seeds, stirring frequently, until seeds are fragrant and dark brown, 7 to 10 minutes. Store in an air-tight container and grind just before using.

Cumin seeds can be toasted several weeks ahead. Chop the onions. Mince the garlic. Drain tomatoes and hominy.

Cut the lamb into chunks and put through a meat grinder, using a plate with ¼-inch holes, or mince by hand. In a heavy saucepan, cook the lamb over medium heat, stirring often, until the meat loses its pink color but is not browned, about 15 minutes. Season to taste with salt and strain off any excess grease.

In another heavy saucepan, heat 2 tablespoons olive oil. Add the onions and garlic, cover, and cook over medium heat, stirring occasionally, until onions are softened, about 10 minutes. Add the onion mixture and canned tomatoes to the lamb, breaking tomatoes up with a large spoon. Add 2 cups water, the cumin, ground chili, allspice, cinnamon, thyme, mustard, and 2 teaspoons of black pepper, and bring to a boil. Reduce heat and simmer, uncovered, stirring occasionally, for 1 hour. Adjust the seasonings.

If the chili seems too thick, add up to ½ cup water. Continue to simmer, stirring often, until the meat is tender, about 30 minutes. If the chili is too thin at the end of cooking, stir in the cornmeal, 1 teaspoon at a time, until the desired thickness is achieved. Simmer for 5 more minutes.

Recipe can be made to this point several days ahead.

COOKING AND SERVING: Reheat the chili if necessary. Seed and mince jalapeno. Melt the butter in a frying pan over medium heat until foamy. Add the jalapeno and salt to taste and cook, stirring occasionally, for 5 minutes. Add the hominy and cook until heated through, 5 to 10 minutes.

Put the hominy into bowls and pour the lamb chili over it, or serve the chili on a platter surrounded by the hominy.

YIELD: 4 servings

Michael McLaughlin
Chef/owner
The Manhattan Chili Company
New York, NY

VINCENT LEE

CAKES AND COOKIES

Crisp Macadamia Wafers

Classic Shortbread

Pop Corriher's Applesauce Cake

The Very Best Angel Food Cake

Raspberry-Steeped Chocolate Cakes

Chocolate Fudge Cake

Chocolate Meringue Cake

Coffee-Cocoa Layer Cake

Crisp Macadamia Wafers

Macadamia nuts give these crisp, delicate wafers their rich taste.

ROASTING AND GRIND-ING NUTS

Roasting vastly improves both the flavor and texture of nuts. Roasting releases their oils (oil accounts for 50 percent of nuts' composition and all of their flavor) and dries them, making them crisper. Oven-roast nuts at about 350°F in a single layer until fragrant and pale golden.

Grinding also releases nuts' oils. Be careful, though, to avoid over-grinding nuts, or they will release so much oil that they will clump together. To keep nuts dry when grinding, add a little of the flour or sugar called for in the recipe.

INGREDIENTS

- 4 ounces macadamia nuts
- 6 ounces softened butter
- ½ cup sugar
- 2 egg whites
- ½ teaspoon vanilla extract
- ½ cup flour

METHOD

PREPARATION: Heat oven to 350°F. Spread nuts in a single layer on a shallow baking sheet and toast until golden brown, about 10 minutes. Cool. Grind ½ of the nuts and chop the remaining ½ into coarse bits. Butter and flour 2 baking sheets.

In a bowl, cream the butter until light. Add the sugar and beat until fluffy. Stir in the egg whites and vanilla. Gently stir in the ground nuts and flour.

Drop batter by teaspoons onto prepared baking sheets, leaving 3 inches between each wafer. Flatten the wafers slightly with the back of a spoon dipped in cold water. Sprinkle each with nuts.

Bake in preheated oven until the wafer edges are golden, 8 to 10 minutes. Transfer to a rack to cool.

Cookies can be made a few days ahead and stored in an airtight container.

SERVING: Serve wafers on their own or with ice cream or espresso.

YIELD: about 4 dozen wafers

VINCENT LEE

Richard Sax
Free-lance writer
New York, NY

Classic Shortbread

It's no wonder the British halt everything for afternoon tea when they have these buttery, crumbly pastries to accompany it.

INGREDIENTS

- ½ **pound softened butter**
- ½ **cup sugar + more for sprinkling**
- 1 **teaspoon vanilla extract**
- ⅛ **teaspoon almond extract**
- 1⅞ **cups all-purpose flour**
- ¼ **cup rice flour or cornstarch**

METHOD

PREPARATION: Cream the butter with ½ cup sugar, the vanilla, and almond extract until the mixture is pale and fluffy, at least 3 minutes.

Whisk or sift together the all-purpose flour and the rice flour. Blend the flours into the creamed mixture until the flour is just incorporated.

Heat oven to 325°F. Divide the dough into 2 parts. Press each portion firmly into a 9- or 10-inch pie plate and smooth the top. With a spatula, draw the edge of each dough round in from the sides, leaving ¼ inch of clear space around the edge of the plate. Use your fingers or the tines of a fork to crimp the edges. If the dough is very soft, chill it. Mark each round into 8 wedges with a knife, cutting the dough only halfway through. If the dough is soft, chill again for 30 minutes. Prick each wedge all the way through in 2 to 3 places with a fork. Alternatively, roll out dough and cut into shapes with a cookie cutter. Sprinkle lightly with sugar.

Bake shortbread in center of preheated oven until creamy golden, not brown, and center is firm to the touch, 25 to 30 minutes. If the shortbread threatens to brown, cover the pan loosely with foil and continue baking until shortbread is firm.

Cool in pans on a rack for 10 minutes. Cut through the scored lines and leave the pieces in the pan until almost cool. Transfer to a rack to cool completely.

Shortbread can be made several days ahead and stored in an airtight tin.

YIELD: 16 wedges

ABOUT SHORTBREAD

Shortbread is the quintessential British pastry. It was originally made from 3 ingredients—butter, sugar and flour, occasionally allowing for a fourth—rice flour. Now, even the staunchest traditionalist is flexible about adding flavors to shortbread, so that it can include caraway, lemon, nuts, spices of all sorts, chocolate, vanilla, ad infinitum.

The rice flour gives shortbread a distinctive texture. It can be found in Oriental or health-food markets. If you cannot find rice flour, substitute cornstarch. Whatever you do, though, don't substitute margarine for the butter. Butter makes the shortbread.

Helen Witty
Free-lance writer
Easthampton, NY

Pop Corriher's Applesauce Cake

An old-fashioned favorite is tailored to modern tastes by reducing the sugar.

VINCENT LEE

INGREDIENTS

       Applesauce, recipe follows
    3 ounces pecans (about ¾ cup chopped)
    2 cups raisins
    3 cups flour
    ½ pound softened butter
    2 cups sugar
    1 teaspoon ground cloves
    1 teaspoon ground allspice
    1 teaspoon ground cinnamon
    ½ teaspoon salt
    2 eggs
    2 teaspoons baking soda
    1 cup heavy cream, optional

METHOD

PREPARATION: Make applesauce.

Heat oven to 350°F. Butter a 10-inch tube pan and line bottom with buttered waxed paper.

Chop the pecans. Dredge raisins in ½ cup flour. Add chopped pecans and set aside. In a large bowl, cream butter and sugar until light and fluffy. Add cloves, allspice, cinnamon, salt and the remaining 2½ cups flour. Gradually fold in raisins and nuts.

Warm the applesauce slightly. In a separate bowl, beat eggs. Mix in applesauce and baking soda. Add applesauce mixture to butter/flour mixture. Mix just to blend.

Pour batter into prepared tube pan and bake in preheated oven until a toothpick inserted in the center comes out clean, about 50 minutes. Be careful not to overcook. Remove from oven and cool on a rack for 10 minutes. Remove cake from mold and cool completely.

Cake can be completed several days ahead.

Whip the cream. This can be done an hour before serving.

SERVING: Cut cake into wedges and serve with whipped cream.

YIELD: 1 cake

Applesauce

INGREDIENTS

    2   pounds apples, such as Rome
          Beauty or McIntosh
          Pinch salt
1 to 2   tablespoons sugar, if necessary

METHOD

PREPARATION: Peel and core the apples and cut them into eighths. In a large, heavy saucepan, put enough water to film the bottom of pan, about 1 tablespoon. Add apples and salt, cover, and bring to a simmer. Raise heat to medium-low and cook, stirring often, until apples are tender, 15 to 20 minutes.

Transfer to a food processor and puree. Add sugar if apples are very tart. Cool slightly before using.

Applesauce can be made a week ahead.

YIELD: about 2 cups

Anne Byrn
Food editor and restaurant
  critic
The Atlanta Journal and
The Atlanta Constitution

The Very Best Angel Food Cake

VINCENT LEE

This cake, with its golden, macaroon-like exterior, will float into your mouth. Only the simplest of garnishes is required—try whipped cream and fresh berries.

INGREDIENTS

1¼	cups cake flour
1¾	cups sugar
12	extra-large egg whites (about 1¾ cups)
1	teaspoon cream of tartar
¼	teaspoon salt
1½	teaspoons vanilla extract
¾	teaspoon almond extract
¾	teaspoon lemon juice
1	cup heavy cream
1	cup berries, such as raspberries, blueberries, blackberries, or a combination

METHOD

PREPARATION: Heat oven to 300°F. Sift the flour and measure 1¼ cups. Sift sugar into a small bowl and set aside. Put egg whites in a large bowl.

Sift cream of tartar over whites, add salt, and beat egg whites to very soft peaks. When bowl is tilted, whites should just flow, not run or slide, out of bowl in a cohesive mass. Sprinkle 2 tablespoons of the sugar over surface of whites and fold in very gently. Repeat until all sugar is thoroughly folded in, using as light a touch as possible. Sift 2 tablespoons of the flour over whites and fold in very gently. Repeat until all flour is incorporated, again using as light a touch as possible. Sprinkle vanilla, almond extract, and lemon juice over batter and fold in gently.

Pour batter into an ungreased 10-inch tube pan with a removable bottom and smooth the top. Rap pan sharply against counter once or twice to remove air bubbles.

Bake in preheated oven until pale brown and springy to the touch, about 1 hour and 10 minutes. Remove from oven, turn pan upside down, and cool in pan 1 hour. If pan has no feet, invert over neck of a bottle.

Cake can be completed a day ahead.

Whip the cream. This can be done an hour ahead.

SERVING: Turn cake right side up and loosen around edges and around central tube with a thin, metal spatula. Remove cake gently from pan. Serve with whipped cream and berries.

YIELD: 1 cake

TAKING THE DEVIL OUT OF ANGEL FOOD CAKE

At its best, angel food cake is light and airy, rising like a cloud out of the pan. However, its virtues make this a very unforgiving cake—there's no disguising an angel food cake that has collapsed.

Two secrets will elevate your angel food cake to new heights: don't overbeat the egg whites and don't bake the cake at too high a temperature. Egg whites should billow rather than form stiff peaks and should roll gently rather than tumble out of the bowl.

The second secret is not to bake at too high a temperature. Since angel food has a high protein content, it tends to toughen, shrink, and dry out when exposed to too much heat. Heat the oven to 300°F for an ethereally light cake.

Jean Anderson
Free-lance writer
New York, NY

Raspberry-Steeped Chocolate Cakes

RICHARD FELBER

These little cakes look pretty and delicate, but they pack a powerfully rich chocolate flavor.

INGREDIENTS

  6¼ ounces semisweet chocolate
  1¼ ounces unsweetened chocolate
  15 tablespoons butter

Raspberry Puree
  1¼ cups fresh raspberries or 7 ounces frozen raspberries
  ½ cup granulated sugar
  1 tablespoon orange liqueur

  5 eggs
  ⅞ cup superfine sugar
  ½ cup cake flour
     Rich Chocolate Glaze, recipe follows
     Decorating Chocolate, recipe follows, optional

METHOD

PREPARATION: Heat oven to 350°F. Butter and flour a 9- by 13-inch baking pan or line it with parchment paper. Chop chocolates into coarse bits and melt in a double boiler set over hot water. Add butter a tablespoon at a time and stir until smooth. Remove from heat. In a food processor, puree the raspberries, granulated sugar, and orange liqueur and strain for Raspberry Puree.

Separate the eggs. Beat the egg yolks with half of the superfine sugar until mixture is light in color and forms a ribbon when trailed from a beater. Stir the chocolate mixture into the yolks. Add the Raspberry Puree to the chocolate/egg yolk mixture.

Beat egg whites until frothy. Add the remaining superfine sugar and beat until soft peaks form. Sift cake flour, measure ½ cup, and fold into the chocolate mixture. Fold in egg whites gently.

Spread batter in prepared pan and smooth top with a spatula. Bake in preheated oven until a toothpick inserted in the center comes out clean, about 25 minutes. Cool.

Put a baking sheet on top of the cooled cake and flip the cake over onto sheet. Cut cake into 8 pieces. Cover with plastic wrap and chill.

Cake can be made to this point a couple of days ahead.

Make the Chocolate Glaze. Make Decorating Chocolate.

Transfer the glaze, a bit at a time, into a small bowl and either spread onto the sides of the cakes with

a spatula or dip the sides of the cakes into the glaze. You may need to warm the glaze to thin it, if dipping. In either case, use a separate bowl to avoid getting crumbs in the remaining glaze to be used for the tops of the cakes.

Put cakes on a rack set over a pan to collect drips. Pour glaze over top of each cake. The glaze should set in about 3 minutes. If desired, make designs on the cakes with Decorating Chocolate using a parchment paper cone.

Cakes can be decorated a day ahead.

SERVING: With a spatula, transfer individual cakes to serving plates.

YIELD: 8 servings

Rich Chocolate Glaze

INGREDIENTS

  ½ pound semisweet chocolate
  ½ pound butter

METHOD

PREPARATION: Chop chocolate into coarse bits and melt in a double boiler set over hot water. Stir in butter a tablespoon at a time. Each piece should partially melt before the next is added. If mixture starts to thin out after you have added about half the butter, remove it from the heat and continue adding the rest of the butter. Make sure butter is thoroughly incorporated and leaves no streaks.

The glaze should be thick enough to set rather quickly but not so thick that it will be difficult to spread a thin layer. To test the consistency, hold some of the glaze above the pan and let it drip back in. It should be visible for 2 to 4 seconds before disappearing into the rest of the glaze. To adjust consistency, let the glaze cool to thicken and heat it gently to thin.

Decorating Chocolate

INGREDIENTS

  2 ounces semisweet or milk chocolate
  ¾ teaspoon oil

METHOD

PREPARATION: Chop chocolate into coarse bits and slowly melt the chocolate in a double boiler set over hot water. Stir in oil. Spoon chocolate into a parchment paper cone (see p.133), fold the top over, and clip off the very end of the tip. Squeeze the bag to get the chocolate flowing and then make a design or border on each cake. Or make the designs first on parchment paper, let set, and transfer to the cake.

Fran Bigelow
Owner/chef
Fran's Patisserie
Seattle, WA

Chocolate Fudge Cake

This superb version of the standard chocolate cake gets its distinctive texture and taste from brown sugar. The frosting is a simple, luscious blend of two chocolates and butter.

INGREDIENTS

Milk-Chocolate Frosting

1	pound milk chocolate
½	pound semisweet or extra-bittersweet chocolate
¾	pound softened butter

Fudge Cake

3	cups cake flour
2	cups light-brown sugar
2¼	teaspoons baking powder
¾	teaspoon baking soda
¾	teaspoon salt
1½	cups milk
3	eggs
1½	teaspoons vanilla extract
4	ounces unsweetened chocolate
6	ounces softened butter

METHOD

PREPARATION: *For the frosting,* chop both chocolates into coarse bits and melt in a double boiler set over hot water. Stir occasionally until completely melted. Remove pan from hot water and allow the chocolate to cool just until no longer warm to the touch, about 20 minutes. Put the butter in a bowl and beat in the cooled chocolate until the mixture is evenly blended, about 3 minutes.

Frosting can be stored at a cool room temperature up to 3 days, or several months in the freezer.

Heat the oven to 350°F. Butter two 9-inch cake pans and line them with buttered and floured parchment paper or waxed paper.

For the Fudge Cake, sift the flour. Measure 3 cups. In a large bowl, mix together the flour, sugar, baking powder, baking soda, and salt, breaking up any lumps of brown sugar.

In a small bowl, whisk about ½ cup of the milk with the eggs and vanilla and set aside. Chop the chocolate into coarse bits and melt in a double boiler set over hot water. Combine the remaining 1 cup milk and the butter with the mixed dry ingredients and beat for 1½ minutes, scraping the sides of the bowl twice. Add the egg mixture in 3 parts, scraping the sides of the bowl and beating for 20 seconds after each addition. Add the melted chocolate and beat just until incorporated.

Pour the batter into the prepared pans and bake in the center of preheated oven until the cake springs back when lightly pressed in the center, 25 to 30 minutes. Cool the cakes in their pans for 10 minutes and invert onto racks. Cool completely before frosting.

Frost the surface of one layer of cake and top with the second layer. Spread the remaining frosting on the sides and top of the cake. Make decorative zigzags in the frosting by pulling a serrated knife across the surface in a back-and-forth motion. Use a small spatula or spoon handle to pull out spikes of frosting all around the sides.

Cake can be completed a day ahead.

SERVING: Return to room temperature if refrigerated. Cut into wedges and serve.

YIELD: one 9-inch cake

For the Chocolate Fudge Cake, *decorate top by using a serrated knife to make zigzag design in frosting.*

Use a small spatula or spoon handle to pull out spikes of frosting all around the sides of cake.

Rose Levy Beranbaum
Free-lance writer
New York, NY

Chocolate Meringue Cake

RICHARD FELBER

This cake is not so difficult to make as it appears, and it's well worth the effort. A crisp, airy meringue is layered with a flaky chocolate pastry and a rich, creamy chocolate ganache. Could there be a better chocolate creation?

MELTING CHOCOLATE

While it may seem painstakingly slow to melt chocolate in a double boiler over hot (not simmering) water, properly melted chocolate is crucial to the finished dessert. If chocolate is melted at too high a temperature, it will lose some of its sheen and texture. When melting chocolate in a double boiler, be sure the water below doesn't exceed 140°F and the top pan doesn't touch the water. You can speed up the process considerably by chopping chocolate into coarse bits first.

You can also melt chocolate in the microwave. Keep in mind that microwaved chocolate will maintain its shape even when it's melted; so don't overheat thinking it hasn't softened yet.

Albert Kumin
Executive chef
International Pastry Arts
  Center
Bedford Hills, NY

INGREDIENTS

Chocolate Meringue
6 egg whites
1¼ cups sugar
¼ pound unsweetened chocolate
⅓ cup water

Chocolate Pastry
¼ pound semisweet chocolate
½ pound butter
1¾ cups flour
¼ teaspoon salt
5 tablespoons cold water

Ganache
10 ounces semisweet chocolate
⅔ cup heavy cream
4 teaspoons butter

4 teaspoons granulated sugar

1 pound semisweet chocolate
½ pound bar semisweet chocolate for curls, optional
Confectioners' sugar for dusting

METHOD

PREPARATION: *For the Chocolate Meringue,* heat the oven to 225°F. Line 2 large baking sheets with parchment paper. Draw two 8-inch circles on each sheet of the parchment paper. Fold the circles in quarters to mark the center.

In a bowl, combine the egg whites with 2 tablespoons sugar and set aside. Chop chocolate into coarse bits. In the top of a double boiler set over hot water, melt the chocolate until lukewarm and set aside. In a small saucepan, combine the remaining 1 cup plus 2 tablespoons sugar and the ⅓ cup water and bring to a boil, brushing any hardened sugar down the side of the pan.

While the syrup is boiling, beat the reserved egg whites to soft peaks. Cook syrup mixture to soft-ball stage (233°F). Add the sugar syrup to the egg whites in a slow stream, beating constantly, and continue to beat slowly until the bowl is cool to the touch. Fold the melted chocolate into meringue.

Fit a pastry bag with ½-inch plain tip and fill with the meringue. On the parchment paper marked with circles, pipe out 2 spirals, starting in the center of each circle and making even 8-inch circles.

To make the strips of meringue edging, fit the pastry bag with a flat, jagged-edged tip with an opening that is ⅞ inch by ¼ inch. Pipe out thin strips of the remaining meringue the length of the other prepared baking sheet. Strips should not touch each other. At least 6 feet of strips are needed to complete the cake.

Bake the meringues in the preheated oven until they start to dry, about 1½ hours. The strips should dry out before the spirals. Turn off the oven and leave meringues in overnight to dry thoroughly. Carefully peel meringues off the parchment paper. If a meringue cracks, it can be put together with ganache during cake assembly. Store the meringues in an airtight tin until ready to use.

Meringue layers can be made up to a week ahead.

For the Chocolate Pastry, chop chocolate into coarse bits and melt in the top of a double boiler set over hot water.

Use a pastry blender or your fingers to work the cold butter into the flour until the pieces are the size of large peas. Make a well in the center of the mixture and add the salt and water. Mix gently until distributed. Incorporate the melted chocolate into the flour mixture until the mixture is crumbly and just forms a ball when lightly pressed together. Set aside for 5 minutes.

Roll the dough out to about a ¼-inch thickness on a floured work surface. Fold into thirds and refrigerate for 10 minutes. Repeat this folding, rolling and chilling process three times. Divide the dough in quarters, cover, and refrigerate for 20 minutes.

On a cool, floured work surface, roll out each quarter of the dough into a round about 9 inches in diameter. Put the rounds on 4 unlined baking sheets and chill for 10 minutes. Prick the surface of the dough thoroughly with a fork.

Heat the oven to 400°F. Bake the pastry in the preheated oven for 8 minutes. Lower the oven temperature to 350°F and bake until just crisp, about 5 more minutes. You may have to bake rounds 2 at a time and repeat with remaining 2 rounds. Carefully remove pastry rounds with a spatula and put on a rack to cool to room temperature. While still warm, trim the Chocolate Pastry into even 8-inch rounds.

Chocolate Pastry can be completed several days ahead.

For the Ganache, chop the chocolate into ½-inch pieces. Combine the cream, butter, and sugar in a saucepan and bring just to a boil. Remove from heat and add the chocolate all at once. Stir until the chocolate has completely melted and the mixture is smooth and well blended. Set aside.

Ganache can be made a couple of days ahead.

Chop the 1 pound of semisweet chocolate into coarse bits and melt in the top of a double boiler over hot water until just lukewarm.

To assemble the cake, carefully coat each layer of Chocolate Pastry with the melted chocolate. Let the chocolate set. Turn the layers over and coat the other sides with chocolate. Let the chocolate set.

Put the first layer of Chocolate Pastry on a cake plate. Cover with ganache, add a meringue layer, and then spread it with ganache. Repeat layering, ending with a pastry layer. Trim any uneven layers carefully with a serrated knife. Cover sides and the top with the remaining ganache. Use a serrated knife to carefully cut the meringue strips into even lengths the height of the cake. Press the meringue strips into place around the cake, completely covering the sides.

For the chocolate curls, warm the chocolate bar by rubbing the top with your hand. Using a long, thin knife, hold both ends at a slight angle to the bar and scrape toward you to form chocolate curls. (If the chocolate is too warm or too cold, it will not form curls.) Place the chocolate curls side-by-side in rows on top of the cake, cutting uneven ends with a knife heated in hot water.

Cut five ½-inch by 8-inch strips of parchment paper, put them diagonally across the top of the cake and dust lightly with confectioners' sugar. Carefully remove the paper strips. Allow the cake to set for 1 to 4 hours at room temperature before serving.

Cake can be assembled a day ahead and refrigerated.

SERVING: Bring back to room temperature before serving if necessary. Cut carefully with a serrated knife.

YIELD: one 8-inch cake

For the Chocolate Meringue Cake, mark 8-inch circles on parchment paper. Pipe meringue in a spiral, starting at the center of each circle.

For the meringue strips, pipe long strips of meringue onto parchment-covered baking sheets, making sure strips don't touch each other.

Trim the layers with a serrated knife to correct any unevenness before covering with ganache.

Coffee-Cocoa Layer Cake

This beautiful cake, layered with coffee and mocha frostings, is an ideal finale to any meal.

For the Coffee-Cocoa Layer Cake, beat the eggs and sugar until they hold a ribbon for two or three seconds.

INGREDIENTS

Sponge Cake

2	tablespoons butter
1½	cups cake flour
⅜	teaspoon salt
7	eggs
1⅛	cups sugar
1¼	teaspoons vanilla

Frostings

2	tablespoons fine-ground coffee beans *or* espresso
1	pound softened butter
⅔	cup confectioners' sugar
3	tablespoons brandy or Cognac
2	tablespoons Dutch-process cocoa
5	tablespoons dry Marsala
½	cup fine-crushed Italian macaroons
1½	cups heavy cream
1½	tablespoons confectioners' sugar
¾	teaspoon vanilla extract

METHOD

PREPARATION: *For the cake,* heat oven to 350°F. Butter two 8-inch-round cake pans, line the bottoms with parchment paper, and flour the sides. Melt the butter and set aside. Sift the cake flour, measure 1½ cups, and combine with salt. In a metal bowl set over warm water, whisk together the eggs and sugar until slightly warm and sugar is dissolved. Remove from pan and beat until eggs trailed from beaters ribbon and hold their shape for 2 or 3 seconds before disappearing. Sift a third of the flour mixture over the egg mixture and fold in gently but thoroughly. Repeat twice with remaining flour. Stir the vanilla into the 2 tablespoons melted butter. Drizzle about ½ the butter over the top of cake batter and fold in. Repeat with the remaining butter. Pour into prepared pans, smooth the top, and bake in preheated oven until the cake is golden and springy to the touch, about 25 minutes. Cool in pans. Remove when cool. Wrap in plastic and let sit overnight.

For the frostings, bring ¼ cup of water to a boil. Grind the coffee beans very fine, put them into a coffee filter over a cup, and pour the boiling water over them. Press gently to extract all liquid. Beat the butter until very light and fluffy. Sift in the confectioners' sugar and beat until light again. Beat in 2 tablespoons of the brandy and the coffee. Set aside ⅓ of the frosting. Sift the cocoa and beat it into the rest of the frosting along with the remaining tablespoon of brandy. Beat well to incorporate all the cocoa.

To assemble the cake, slice each of the cakes into 3 thin, even layers. Set the bottom layer on a plate and brush it lightly with 1 tablespoon of the Marsala. Spread a very thin layer of the plain coffee frosting over the cake layer. Set the next layer on top, brush with 1 tablespoon Marsala, and spread a very thin layer of the mocha frosting. Repeat with the remaining layers, brushing each layer with 1 tablespoon Marsala and alternating coffee and mocha frostings. Reserve about half of the mocha frosting and leave top and sides unfrosted. Chill cake at least overnight.

Cake can be made and filled 2 days ahead.

Soften and beat remaining mocha frosting. Spread a thin layer of the mocha frosting on the sides and top of the cake. Crush the macaroons and dust over the edge of the cake. Let the cake stand at room temperature for at least 2 hours before serving.

Cake can be frosted a day ahead.

Whip the cream and flavor to taste with confectioners' sugar and vanilla. This can be done an hour ahead.

SERVING: Cut cake into wedges and serve with whipped cream.

YIELD: 12 servings

Lindsey Shere
Pastry chef
Chez Panisse
Berkeley, CA

RICHARD FELBER

TARTS

Mango Tart with Lime

Mellow mango and tart lime are set off nicely by sweet pastry cream in this tart.

PASTRY CREAM

Pastry cream is another French classic (crème pâtissière). Pastry cream is often flavored with a fruit alcohol such as kirsch, which goes nicely with all kinds of fruit. You can vary the flavoring according to the fruit used in the tart or your own taste. When making pastry cream ahead, press plastic directly on the surface of the cream so that no skin forms and then refrigerate. Pastry cream can be made a few days in advance.

INGREDIENTS

1   recipe Sweet Pastry (page 136)
1   recipe Pastry Cream (page 136)
1   cup apricot preserves
1   lime
2   mangoes

METHOD

PREPARATION: Make the Sweet Pastry. Make the Pastry Cream. Make a glaze by heating the apricot preserves with 1 teaspoon water over low heat until dissolved. Strain.

Recipe can be made to this point a few days ahead.

Roll out dough to measure slightly larger than an 8- or 9-inch tart pan. Line the pan with the dough. Gently press the dough on the bottom of the pan toward the middle. Press the dough down around the sides so that just a fraction of an inch extends above the tart pan. Roll a rolling pin across the top to cut off excess dough. Prick bottom thoroughly with a fork, line with buttered aluminum foil, shiny side down, and fill with dry beans or pie weights. Chill at least 15 minutes or even overnight.

Heat oven to 375°F. Bake tart crust in preheated oven 10 minutes and then lower temperature to 350°F. Bake 10 minutes more and remove foil and beans. Return to oven until dough is dry and lightly browned, about 10 additional minutes.

Tart crust can be baked a day ahead.

Reheat apricot glaze if necessary. With a zesting tool, remove lime zest in long, thin strips. If you don't have a zester, use the finest hole on a grater.

Peel and pit the mangoes and cut them into thin slices. Squeeze juice from the lime over mangoes.

Fill the tart shell with the Pastry Cream. Arrange the mango slices in an overlapping spiral on top of the Pastry Cream and brush the fruit with the apricot glaze. Pile lime zest in the center or sprinkle tart with grated zest.

Recipe can be completed a few hours ahead.

SERVING: Unmold the tart, cut into slices, and serve.

YIELD: One 8- or 9-inch tart

For the Mango Tart, remove the tart shell from the tin most easily by putting the center of the tin over a round object, such as a coffee can. The ring will fall away.

Cut the fruit and push gently to flatten into a row of overlapping slices. Use a spatula to place on the pastry cream.

Chocolate-Dipped Strawberry Tartlets

These beautiful little tartlets are the stuff romance is made of.

NANCY McFARLAND

INGREDIENTS

1	recipe Sweet Pastry (page 136)
1	recipe Pastry Cream (page 136)
1	pint strawberries
¼	pound semisweet chocolate
¼	pound butter

METHOD

PREPARATION: Make the Sweet Pastry. Make the Pastry Cream.

Divide dough into 6 pieces and roll each piece out to measure slightly larger than a 4-inch tartlet pan. Gently press each round of dough on the bottom of the pan toward the middle. Press the dough down around the sides so they extend just slightly above the tartlet pans. Roll a rolling pin across tops to cut off excess dough. Prick bottoms thoroughly with a fork, line with buttered foil, shiny side down, and fill with beans or pie weights. Chill at least 15 minutes or overnight.

Heat oven to 375°F. Bake 5 minutes, then lower temperature to 350°F. Bake 5 more minutes and remove foil and beans. Return to oven until dough is dry and lightly browned, 8 additional minutes.

Tartlet shells can be baked a day ahead.

Hull and halve the strawberries. Chop chocolate into coarse bits and melt with butter in the top of a double boiler set over hot water. Using a pastry brush, paint the top rim of the tartlet crusts with the melted chocolate. Fill tartlets with Pastry Cream. Dip the strawberries halfway into the chocolate and put on a piece of waxed paper to set. Arrange the strawberries inside each tartlet on top of the Pastry Cream with tips pointed up.

Tartlets can be made a few hours ahead.

SERVING: Unmold tartlets and serve.

YIELD: Six 4-inch tartlets

Beaujolais Pear Tart

RICHARD FELBER

All but the final assembly of this stunning tart can be done as much as several days before serving.

PASTRY CRUST

This sweet pastry is based on the classic French pâte sucrée. While the French method calls for blending the butter completely into the flour for a smooth dough, this Americanized version leaves bits of butter intact for a flakier crust.

Lindsey Shere
Pastry chef
Chez Panisse
Berkeley, CA

INGREDIENTS

Beaujolais Poached Pears
1 2-inch piece vanilla bean
2 cups light red wine, such as Beaujolais or Zinfandel
1 cup water
1 cup sugar
2 strips orange zest
1 strip lemon zest
4 small Bosc pears (about 1¼ pounds)

1 recipe Sweet Pastry (page 136)

Apple Puree
4 cooking apples, such as McIntosh (about 1½ pounds)
2 tablespoons water
1 tablespoon butter
1 cinnamon stick

Caramelized Walnuts
½ cup walnut halves
1 tablespoon water

½ cup sugar
  Few drops lemon juice

1 teaspoon kirsch

METHOD

PREPARATION: *For the poached pears,* split the vanilla bean and scrape seeds into a saucepan. Add the wine, water, sugar, and orange and lemon zests and bring to a simmer. Peel, core, and halve the pears and add to the simmering liquid. Cook over medium-high heat until just tender, about 15 minutes, depending on variety and ripeness of pears. Chill the pears in their poaching liquid.

  Make the pastry. Roll out dough to measure slightly larger than an 8- or 9-inch tart pan. Gently press the dough on the bottom of the pan toward the middle. Press the dough down around the sides so that just a fraction of an inch extends above the tart pan. Roll a rolling pin across the top to cut off excess dough. Prick bottom thoroughly with a fork, line with buttered aluminum foil, shiny side down, and fill with dry beans or pie weights. Chill at least 15 minutes or even overnight.

For the Apple Puree, peel, quarter, core, and slice the apples. In a saucepan, combine the apples, water, butter, and cinnamon stick, cover, and cook over low heat, stirring often, until the apples form a thick puree, about 30 minutes. Remove cinnamon stick. Chill.

For the Caramelized Walnuts, heat oven to 350°F. Toast walnuts in preheated oven for about 10 minutes. Cool and rub off any loose skins. Butter a plate large enough to hold the walnuts in a single layer. Put water, sugar, and lemon juice in a saucepan and cook over low heat, swirling pan gently to cook sugar evenly until it turns a golden caramel color, about 7 minutes. Remove caramel from heat. Using a fork, quickly dip the walnuts, one by one, into hot caramel to coat with a thin layer and transfer to the buttered plate. If caramel gets too thick, reheat over low heat before continuing. Quarter walnuts and keep in an airtight container.

Recipe can be made to this point a few days ahead.

Heat oven to 375°F. Bake the prepared, chilled tart shell in preheated oven for 10 minutes. Reduce heat to 350°F and bake for 10 more minutes. Remove foil and beans and bake until golden, about 10 additional minutes.

Tart shell can be baked a day ahead.

Drain the pears, reserving poaching liquid. To make a sauce, cook 1½ cups of the poaching liquid over high heat until slightly syrupy, about 25 minutes. Add the kirsch and flame.

Fill the baked shell with the apple puree and smooth the top. Push the walnuts into the apple filling. Slice the poached pears and arrange over the top of filling.

Tart can be completed a few hours before serving.

SERVING: Reheat the sauce. Cut tart into slices and serve with a little warm sauce on the side.

YIELD: One 8- or 9-inch tart

Caramel Pecan Tartlets

RICHARD FELBER

Other nuts besides pecans can be used in these tarts. Or a combination of pecans, walnuts, and hazelnuts is especially attractive.

SUCCESSFUL CARAMEL MAKING

Caramel making may seem pretty daunting to the inexperienced candy maker, but a few rules will help you on your way to success.
- **Never stir before all the sugar is dissolved, or it can crystallize.**
- **Keep your eye on it—once the sugar begins to color, it can burn in a flash.**
- **Be sure your pan is big enough since sugar can bubble to four times its original volume.**
- **Keep a larger pan of cold water next to the stove to stop the cooking immediately when it reaches the right color. As you get more experienced, you'll be able to pull the sugar off the stove before it's ready and let the residual pan heat finish the job.**

Fran Bigelow
Owner/chef
Fran's Patisserie and
  Chocolate Specialties
Seattle, WA

INGREDIENTS

1 recipe Sweet Pastry (page 136)
6 ounces pecans, walnuts, and/or hazelnuts (about 1½ cups)

Soft Caramel
¾ cup sugar
¾ cup water
7 tablespoons heavy cream, approximately

1 cup heavy cream
2 teaspoons sugar
½ teaspoon vanilla

METHOD

PREPARATION: Make Sweet Pastry.

Heat oven to 350°F. Spread nuts in a single layer on a shallow baking sheet and toast, stirring occasionally, until fragrant and lightly browned, about 10 minutes.

For the Soft Caramel, combine sugar and ¾ cup water in a heavy saucepan and cook over low heat until water turns clear, about 10 minutes. Do not stir. Raise heat to high and boil until mixture turns a golden brown, about 15 minutes. To prevent crystallization, wash sugar crystals from the side of the pan with a wet pastry brush as sugar mixture boils. Remove from heat and add the cream slowly and carefully, as it will bubble up and spatter. With a long-handled spoon, stir to combine. To test caramel consistency, put a small amount on a plate and let cool. If, when touched, caramel is too soft,

continue cooking, being careful it doesn't get any darker than caramel color. If the caramel is too hard, add more cream. Put pan into a cold-water bath to stop cooking.

Recipe can be made to this point several days ahead.

Divide the dough into six pieces and roll out to measure slightly larger than six 4-inch tartlet pans. Gently press each round of dough on the bottom of the pan toward the middle. Press the dough down around the sides so that just a fraction of an inch extends above the tartlet pans. Roll a rolling pin across the tops to cut off excess dough. Prick bottoms thoroughly with a fork, line with buttered aluminum foil, shiny side down, and fill each with dry beans or pie weights. Chill at least 15 minutes or even overnight.

Heat oven to 375°F. Bake in preheated oven 5 minutes and then lower temperature to 350°F. Bake 5 minutes more and remove foil and beans. Return to oven until dough is dry and lightly browned, about 8 additional minutes.

Rewarm the caramel slowly in a double boiler over low heat and add the nuts. Stir thoroughly and divide among the tartlet shells.

Recipe can be completed a day ahead.

Whip the cream with the sugar and vanilla.

Cream can be whipped an hour ahead and refrigerated.

SERVING: Unmold tartlets and top with whipped cream before serving if desired.

YIELD: Six 4-inch tartlets

130

Pear Mincement Tart

The pear mincemeat tart is considerably lighter than the traditional mincemeat and is set off with a pretty pinwheel of sliced pears.

INGREDIENTS

Pear Mincement

2	firm pears, such as bosc
¼	cup raisins
⅓	cup brown sugar
½	cup dry white wine
¼	teaspoon cinnamon
⅛	teaspoon ground cloves
¼	teaspoon ground nutmeg
¼	teaspoon ground ginger
2	tablespoons butter
1	tablespoon brandy
1	recipe Sweet Pastry (page 136)
¼	cup ginger preserves *or* apple jelly
4 to 5	firm pears, such as bosc
½	lemon
2	tablespoons sugar
1	cup heavy cream
½	teaspoon brandy
	Nutmeg for sprinkling

METHOD

PREPARATION: *For the Pear Mincemeat,* peel, core, and chop the pears. In a saucepan, combine pears, raisins, brown sugar, and wine. Bring to a boil and simmer, partially covered, until pears are tender and liquid is reduced by half, about 40 minutes. Add cinnamon, cloves, nutmeg, ginger, butter, and brandy. Cook 5 more minutes.

Mincemeat can be made ahead and stored in the refrigerator for at least 5 days.

Make the Sweet Pastry.

To make a glaze, heat the ginger preserves or apple jelly with 1 teaspoon of water over low heat until dissolved. Strain if using preserves.

Recipe can be made to this point a few days ahead.

Peel and core pears and cut lengthwise into ¼- to ½-inch slices. Squeeze lemon juice over slices and toss.

On a floured work surface, roll out pastry to measure slightly larger than a 9-inch tart pan. Gently press the dough on the bottom of the pan toward the middle. Press the dough down around the sides so that just a fraction of an inch extends above pan. Roll over top of pan with a rolling pin to trim crust. Prick bottom of tart shell thoroughly. Chill 15 minutes.

Reheat glaze if necessary.

Heat oven to 375°F. Spread mincemeat on bottom of shell. Arrange pear slices in concentric circles, starting from outside edge and overlapping slightly to form 2 or 3 rings of pear slices, using smaller slices toward the center of tart. Sprinkle with 1½ tablespoons sugar.

Bake tart in preheated oven until crust is golden brown and pears are tender, about 1 hour. Cool.

Brush glaze over cooled tart.

Tart can be completed a day ahead.

Whip the cream with the remaining sugar and brandy. This can be done an hour ahead.

SERVING: Slice the tart and serve with a dollop of whipped cream sprinkled with nutmeg.

YIELD: One 9-inch tart

For the Pear Mincemeat Tart, arrange pear slices in concentric circles starting from the outside and overlapping slightly.

Jane Stacey
Free-lance food writer and
	caterer
Albuquerque, NM

Jam Tart

PREBAKING THE CRUST

When putting the dough into the pan, ease it in. Don't stretch the crust, or it will shrink in the oven. Press the dough on the bottom of the pan toward the middle and push excess dough down the sides—the crust is less likely to shrink this way. Trim off excess dough from edges by rolling a rolling pin along the top.

Prick the dough thoroughly so that the crust won't bubble up. Line crust with buttered aluminum foil, shiny side down, and fill with dry beans or pie weights. Chill for at least 15 minutes or even overnight to firm. Put crust directly into hot oven and cook for 10 minutes, reduce heat and bake another 10 minutes, then remove weights and foil and finish baking until golden.

This country-style tart filled with jam and topped with a pastry lattice is easy to make. Since quite a bit of jam is used, a low-sugar jam is a good choice.

INGREDIENTS

1 recipe Sweet Pastry (page 136)
2 cups low-sugar jam, such as strawberry or raspberry
1 egg

METHOD

PREPARATION AND COOKING: Make the Sweet Pastry.

Butter and flour a 9-inch tart pan. On a floured work surface, roll ⅔ of the dough to measure slightly larger than the pan. Line the pan with the dough. Gently press the dough on the bottom of the pan toward the middle. Press dough down around the sides so that just a fraction of an inch extends above the tart pan. Roll a rolling pin across the top to cut off the excess dough, reserving scraps. Prick bottom thoroughly with a fork. Fill crust with jam.

Roll out remaining ⅓ dough to a 10-inch-long rectangle and cut dough lengthwise into 10 even strips. Put 5 strips over top of tart at even intervals. Place remaining 5 strips across those on tart to form lattice. Pinch ends of strips to bottom crust. Lightly beat egg and brush over lattice strips.

Heat oven to 375°F. Bake on lowest rack in preheated oven until crust is golden, about 30 minutes.

Tart can be made a day ahead.

SERVING: Unmold the tart and cut into slices.

YIELD: one 9-inch tart

Jane Freiman
Contributing editor
NEW YORK Magazine

Chocolate-Coated Walnut Caramel Tart

RICHARD FELBER

Beauty is not just skin deep in this tart—beneath the rich, elegant chocolate ganache coating lies a moist caramel filling studded with crisp walnuts.

To make a parchment cone, cut a piece of paper in half diagonally. Overlap the two sharper points to form a cone.

With thumbs inside the cone and fingers outside, slide the sharper points toward the center one.

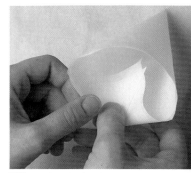

When the tip is tight and sharp, fold the points inside the cone to secure it.

INGREDIENTS

1   recipe Sweet Pastry (page 136)

Walnut Caramel Filling
½   pound walnuts (about 2 cups)
6½ tablespoons butter
1   cup sugar
1   cup water
⅞   cup cream

1   egg yolk

Ganache
¼   pound semisweet chocolate
¼   cup heavy cream
1½ tablespoons butter

2   ounces white chocolate, for optional decoration
1   tablespoon oil, for optional decoration

METHOD

PREPARATION: Make the Sweet Pastry. Divide the dough into two discs, one slightly larger than the other. Cover with plastic wrap and refrigerate.

For the filling, chop the walnuts. Cut butter into ½-inch cubes. In a saucepan, bring sugar and 1 cup of water to a boil and cook until it turns into a light golden caramel, about 10 minutes. Slowly pour the cream into boiling liquid, being careful not to spatter. Stir in the walnuts and butter cubes. Cook mixture on high heat, stirring to prevent burning the walnuts, until syrup is reduced and is a rich caramel color, about 7 minutes. Pour into bowl and cool to room temperature.

Pastry and filling can be made a few days ahead.

Roll larger disc of dough out to measure slightly larger than an 8- or 9-inch tart pan. Gently press the dough on the bottom of the pan toward the middle, and press dough down around the sides so it extends just a fraction of an inch above the tart pan.

Roll a rolling pin over top of tart pan to trim crust. Prick bottom of crust thoroughly with a fork. Cover tart shell with plastic wrap and chill until ready to assemble, at least 15 minutes or even overnight.

Heat oven to 375°F. Mix egg yolk with 2 teaspoons water for egg wash. Brush around the edges of the pastry shell with the egg wash. Gently spread cooled, caramelized walnuts over entire shell, being careful not to rip the pastry. Roll out smaller disc of dough to about ⅛-inch thick and 9½-inches wide. Top tart with pastry and pinch top and bottom crusts together. Seal and trim by rolling over the rim of the pan with a rolling pin.

Bake tart pastry on bottom rack in preheated oven until the crust turns golden brown, about 40 minutes. If it browns before 40 minutes, cover lightly with foil.

Recipe can be made to this point a day ahead.

For the Ganache, chop chocolate into coarse bits and melt with cream and butter in a double boiler over hot water, stirring constantly, until smooth.

Unmold tart onto serving plate and spread top and sides with the ganache.

For optional decoration, chop white chocolate into coarse bits and melt with oil over water in a double boiler until almost melted. Remove from heat and stir until completely melted. Make a small parchment cone (see cake decorating instructions on this page). Scrape white chocolate into cone. When ganache is almost set, pipe a spiral design on top of tart. When white-chocolate spiral is almost set, make 8 "spokes" by dragging a paring knife from the center of the tart to the edges. Then make 8 more spokes in between each, this time moving from the edges toward the center. The design should resemble a spider's web.

Recipe can be completed a day ahead.

SERVING: Cut tart into thin slices and serve.

YIELD: One 8- or 9-inch tart

Michael McCarty
Owner
Michael's Restaurant
Santa Monica, CA

Chocolate-Covered Bavarian

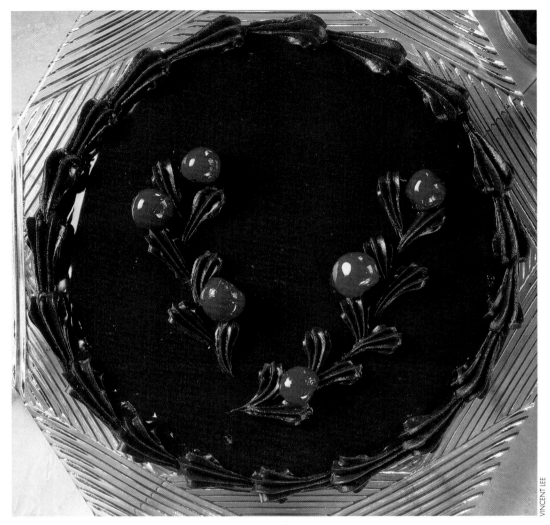

Chocolate lovers will rejoice over this rich chocolate-cherry dessert that can be made a day ahead.

VINCENT LEE

INGREDIENTS

Cherries
1   1-pound can Morello or Bing cherries in syrup
¼   cup sugar
¼   cup kirsch or brandy

Chocolate Cookie Crust
3   ounces semisweet chocolate
12 ounces chocolate wafers

Chocolate Bavarois
2   ounces extra-bittersweet chocolate
3   egg yolks
½   cup sugar
2   teaspoons unflavored gelatin
1   cup milk
¼   teaspoon vanilla extract
⅔   cup heavy cream
4   teaspoons kirsch or brandy

Glaze
7   ounces semisweet chocolate
½   cup + 2 tablespoons heavy cream

Corn syrup for glazing the cherries

Rose Levy Beranbaum
Free-lance writer
New York, NY

METHOD

PREPARATION: *For the cherries,* drain the cherries at least 12 hours ahead, reserving ½ cup of the syrup. In a saucepan, combine the syrup, ½ cup water, and the ¼ cup sugar and bring to a boil, stirring. Add the cherries, cover, and simmer for 1 minute. Remove from the heat and add the kirsch. Cover and let stand for 12 to 24 hours.

Cherries can be prepared several months ahead and refrigerated.

Remove the cherries from the liquid and drain thoroughly on paper towels.

For the crust, chop the semisweet chocolate into coarse bits and melt in the top of a double boiler set over hot water. Whir the cookies in a food processor until they are fine crumbs and add the chocolate. Add 1 tablespoon of water and process for a few seconds. Line a 10-inch pie pan with aluminum foil so that the foil extends beyond the rim. Press the crumbs into the pan, making the bottom as thin as possible and building up the sides. Put all but 6 drained cherries into the shell and refrigerate until the filling is prepared.

For the Chocolate Bavarois, grate the bittersweet

134

chocolate into a bowl. In another mixing bowl, combine the egg yolks with ¼ cup of the sugar and the gelatin. Beat until double in volume. In a saucepan, bring the milk and remaining ¼ cup of sugar to a boil. Gradually add the hot milk to the egg yolks to temper them, whisking constantly. Return the mixture to the pan and cook over low heat, stirring constantly with a wooden spoon, until it thickens just enough to coat the back of a spoon lightly or until it reaches 160°F on a thermometer, about 10 minutes. Do not boil. Remove immediately from the heat and strain into the grated chocolate, stirring until the chocolate is completely melted. Add the vanilla.

Whip the cream. Set the bowl of chocolate mixture in a larger bowl or pan of ice water and whisk until it starts to set around the edges. Whisk in the kirsch and one quarter of the whipped cream. Fold in the remaining whipped cream. Remove from the ice water and pour the Bavarois over the cherries in the pie shell. Cover with plastic wrap and refrigerate until set, at least 1 hour.

Recipe can be made to this point a couple of days ahead.

For the glaze, grate 6 ounces of the chocolate. Bring the cream almost to a boil, remove from heat, and add the grated chocolate. Stir gently until it is fully melted and the mixture is smooth. If necessary, heat slightly, being careful not to incorporate any air bubbles. Cool just until tepid. Pour about half of the glaze onto the pie. Using a long, metal spatula, smooth evenly onto the surface. Refrigerate until set before decorating, at least 1 hour.

Use the foil to lift the dessert out of the pan. Peel off the foil and put Chocolate-Covered Bavarian on a serving platter. Chop the remaining 1 ounce of chocolate into coarse bits, melt in a double boiler set over hot water, and stir into the remaining glaze. Set the bowl of glaze over ice and stir gently just until the glaze is thick enough for piping. Do not beat the glaze or it will lighten in color.

To decorate the pie, put the glaze in a pastry bag fitted with a ¼-inch star tip. Pipe a border around the edge of the crust. Brush the reserved cherries lightly with corn syrup and arrange on top of the pie. Pipe decorative leaves for the cherries. Refrigerate for at least 1 hour to set.

Dessert can be completed a day ahead.

SERVING: Cut into wedges with a sharp knife that has been dipped in hot water and dried. Support the rim with one hand while cutting.

YIELD: 8 servings

Sweet Pastry

INGREDIENTS

- 1¼ cups all-purpose flour
- ¼ cup cake flour
- ¼ cup sugar
- ¼ teaspoon salt
- ¼ pound butter
- 2 egg yolks
- Water, if necessary

METHOD

PREPARATION: Mix the flours, sugar, and salt in a bowl. Butter should be thoroughly chilled. Either cut it in or work it in with your fingers until mixture resembles coarse meal with some pea-size pieces of butter remaining. Work in the egg yolks, and add up to 3 tablespoons of water, if necessary, to hold dough together. Press the dough into a ball, cover with plastic wrap, and chill at least 20 minutes before rolling.

Dough can be refrigerated for a few days but should be brought to room temperature before rolling.

YIELD: Dough for 1 tart or 6 tartlets

Pastry Cream

INGREDIENTS

- 2½ tablespoons flour
- ¼ cup sugar
- Pinch of salt
- 3 egg yolks
- 1 cup milk
- 2 teaspoons butter
- 1 teaspoon vanilla
- 1½ tablespoons liqueur or eau de vie

METHOD

PREPARATION: Combine flour, sugar, and salt together in a heavy pan. Beat in egg yolks. Gradually add the milk. Whisk over low heat until mixture is thick and large bubbles break the surface, about 3 minutes. Boil 1 minute, stirring constantly. Remove from heat and stir in the butter, vanilla, and a liqueur or eau de vie that complements the fruit you're using. Cover with plastic wrap and chill.

The pastry cream can be made a few days in advance.

YIELD: Enough pastry cream for 1 tart or 6 tartlets

OTHER DESSERTS

Apple and Cider Soup with Raisins

Plum Ice Cream with Strawberries

Pecan-Pie Ice Cream and Pie-Pastry Cookies

Peaches and Cream on Almond Meringues

Montrachet Cheesecake

Cranberry and Mango Cobbler with Cinnamon and Pecan Cream

Chocolate Truffles

Pineapple Pastry with Caramel Sauce

Chocolate Pots de Crème

Chocolate Mousse

Chocolate Soufflé

Profiteroles

Apple and Cider Soup with Raisins

Soup, a soothing way to begin a meal, is an exciting way to finish one. This dessert soup combines rustic ingredients—white bread, apples, raisins, and brown sugar—for a dessert that is satisfying but sophisticated.

INGREDIENTS

3	slices white bread
3	tablespoons butter
¼	cup rice
2¾	cups apple cider
2	cooking apples, such as McIntosh
½	cup raisins
2	tablespoons applejack or apple schnapps to taste
¼	teaspoon cinnamon
¼	teaspoon nutmeg + more for garnish, if desired
1	tablespoon brown sugar, approximately
½	cup heavy cream
2	teaspoons sugar
¼	teaspoon vanilla extract

METHOD

PREPARATION: Trim crusts from bread and cut into ¼-inch cubes. In a large frying pan, sauté bread cubes over medium heat in 2 tablespoons of the butter, turning frequently, until golden brown, 1 to 2 minutes. Drain.

Croutons can be made several days ahead and stored in an airtight container.

In a small saucepan, melt remaining tablespoon butter. Stir in rice. Add 1¾ cups of the cider and bring to a simmer. Cover and cook until liquid is absorbed and rice is tender, about 20 minutes. Set aside, covered, for 10 minutes.

Peel, quarter, and core the apples. Cut into ⅛-inch-thick slices and add to rice along with raisins, ¼ cup water, remaining 1 cup cider, applejack, cinnamon, and ¼ teaspoon nutmeg. Bring to a simmer and add about 1 tablespoon brown sugar or to taste. Cook over medium heat until apples are just tender, about 3 minutes.

Soup can be completed several hours ahead.

Whip cream with sugar and vanilla until it holds firm peaks. Refrigerate.

Whipped cream can be made an hour ahead.

SERVING: Reheat soup if needed. Pour into bowls. Top with a dollop of whipped cream and sprinkle with croutons and a pinch of nutmeg if desired.

YIELD: 4 servings

Pamela Parseghian
Food editor
COOK'S Magazine

Plum Ice Cream with Strawberries

Plums lend their vivid color and summer-ripe flavor to an uncommonly good ice cream. You can experiment with any of the wide variety of plums available; all give wonderful results.

INGREDIENTS

Plum Ice Cream
5	soft, ripe plums (¾ to 1 pound)
2	egg yolks
1⅛	cups heavy cream
¾	cup sugar
½	teaspoon vanilla extract, approximately
½	teaspoon kirsch, approximately
1	pint strawberries
2	tablespoons sugar, approximately

METHOD

PREPARATION: *For the ice cream,* halve and pit plums. Put them in a nonreactive saucepan with ¼ cup water. Cover and bring plums to a simmer. Cook gently over medium-low heat, stirring occasionally to keep them from sticking, until they are tender, 10 to 15 minutes. Puree plums, including skins and cooking liquid, until almost smooth, and let cool.

Lightly beat the egg yolks. Heat the heavy cream with ¾ cup sugar until sugar melts, about 5 minutes over low heat. Gradually beat warm mixture into egg yolks to temper them. Return cream mixture to the pan and cook over very low heat, stirring constantly, until slightly thickened and coats the back of a spoon (160°F), about 10 minutes. Immediately strain into a container and add plum puree. Flavor with vanilla and kirsch to taste and freeze in an ice-cream machine according to manufacturer's instructions.

Ice cream can be completed several days ahead.

Hull and slice the strawberries and add sugar to taste. Cover and let stand at room temperature at least ½ hour. Strawberries can be prepared several hours ahead.

SERVING: Serve plum ice cream with the sugared strawberries and their juices.

YIELD: 4 servings

For the Plum Ice Cream, puree simmered plums with their skins and cooking liquid until almost smooth.

Lindsey Shere
Pastry chef
Chez Panisse
Berkeley, CA

Pecan-Pie Ice Cream and Pie-Pastry Cookies

NANCY McFARLAND

This ice cream dessert delights in the same way traditional pie and ice cream does, and yet seems refreshingly cool and light.

FREEZING ICE CREAM

Once the ice cream has frozen, let it "ripen" in the refrigerator freezer for 2 to 3 hours for best flavor. You can leave it in the cannister, if it's removable, or pack it into a metal bowl and cover tightly with plastic wrap. Since home-made ice cream contains no preservatives or stabilizers, it is best when eaten within a week.

INGREDIENTS

1   recipe Basic Vanilla Ice Cream, recipe
    follows
    Pie-Pastry Cookies, recipe follows
2   eggs
6   ounces pecans (about 1¼ cups
    chopped + ¼ cup pecan halves)
½   cup sugar
¼   cup dark corn syrup
3½ tablespoons butter

METHOD

PREPARATION: Make the Vanilla Ice Cream. Make the Pie-Pastry Cookies.

Heat the oven to 350°F. Butter a 10-inch pie plate. Put the eggs in a bowl and beat lightly. Chop 1¼ cups pecans. In a small saucepan, combine the sugar, corn syrup, and 2 tablespoons of the butter.

Bring to a boil, stirring constantly, until the mixture is melted and smooth. Slowly pour the hot syrup in a thin stream into the bowl with the beaten eggs, whisking constantly. Add the chopped pecans and stir well.

Pour into the prepared pie plate and bake in preheated oven until browned and a knife inserted in the center comes out clean, about 40 minutes. Cool and cut into small pieces.

Spread a 1-inch layer of ice cream in a baking dish. Distribute half the baked pecan mixture over the ice cream. Spread another 1-inch layer of ice cream over it, layer with the remaining pecan filling mixture, and finish with another layer of ice cream. If the ice cream begins to melt while you are working, put it back in the freezer until firm again. Cover with plastic wrap. Freeze until firm.

Heat remaining 1½ tablespoons butter in a frying pan. Add the pecan halves and stir over medium-

Pamela Parseghian
Food editor
COOK'S Magazine

high heat to toast lightly.

Recipe can be completed 2 days ahead.

SERVING: Scoop the ice cream into chilled glasses, top each serving with sautéed pecans, and serve with pie-pastry cookies.

YIELD: 6 servings

Basic Vanilla Ice Cream

INGREDIENTS

- 1 **vanilla bean** *or* **1½ teaspoons vanilla extract**
- 2 **cups milk**
- 2 **cups heavy cream**
- 8 **egg yolks**
- ¼ **cup sugar**

METHOD

PREPARATION: Split the vanilla bean, if using, and put in a saucepan with the milk and heavy cream. Bring just to a boil over medium heat.

In a bowl, beat the egg yolks with the sugar until they are thick and pale yellow in color. Whisk in the hot milk mixture and then pour mixture back into the saucepan. Warm over low heat, stirring constantly, until the mixture begins to thicken slightly and coats the back of a spoon, about 10 minutes (160°F). Be careful not to boil or the mixture will curdle.

Remove from heat, stir in vanilla extract, if using, and strain the mixture through a sieve lined with several layers of cheesecloth or a coffee filter. Scrape the seeds from the vanilla bean into the custard and stir. Lay plastic wrap directly on the surface to prevent a skin from forming. Cool completely.

Transfer the mixture to an ice-cream maker and freeze according to the manufacturer's instructions.

Ice cream can be made several days ahead.

YIELD: 1 to 1½ quarts

Pie-Pastry Cookies

INGREDIENTS

- 6 **tablespoons butter**
- 1 **egg yolk**
- 1¼ **cups flour**
  Pinch of salt
- 1½ **tablespoons sugar + more for sprinkling cookies**

METHOD

PREPARATION: Cut well chilled butter into small pieces. Beat egg yolk with 2 tablespoons cold water. In a bowl, combine the flour, salt, and 1½ tablespoons sugar. Work the butter into the flour, using your fingertips or a pastry blender, until the mixture is the consistency of coarse meal with a few pea-size pieces of butter remaining. Make a well in the center of the butter-flour mixture. Pour in the egg yolk mixture and combine. Gather the dough into a ball.

Flour the heel of your hand. On a work surface, smear dough a handful at a time away from you to complete blending. Gather the dough together with a pastry scraper, form into a ball, and wrap in plastic wrap. Refrigerate for at least 30 minutes.

Heat the oven to 375°F.

On a lightly floured work surface, roll out the pastry dough into a 10-inch square that is approximately ¼ inch thick. Trim the edges and cut the dough into four 2½-inch-wide strips. Cut the strips into pie-wedge shapes about 1½ inches wide. Put the triangles on an ungreased baking sheet. Flute the top edge of each triangle with your fingertips or a pastry crimper to resemble a piecrust. Sprinkle with sugar.

Bake in preheated oven until golden around the edges, 8 to 10 minutes. Cool on a rack. Store in an airtight container.

Cookies can be completed 2 days ahead.

YIELD: 32 cookies

Peaches and Cream on Almond Meringues

Elizabeth Riely
Free-lance writer
Newton Centre, MA

VINCENT LEE

Sweet, juicy peaches combine with crisp, airy meringues in this luscious dessert.

INGREDIENTS

Almond Meringues
- 3 ounces blanched almonds (about ⅔ cup)
- 3 large egg whites
  Salt
- 1 cup confectioners' sugar
- ⅛ teaspoon vanilla extract

- 1½ cups granulated sugar
- ¼ teaspoon vanilla extract
- 3 large peaches
- 1 cup heavy cream
- 2 teaspoons sugar
- 1 tablespoon Amaretto or kirsch
  Nutmeg for sprinkling

METHOD

PREPARATION: *For the Almond Meringues,* heat oven to 350°F. Spread the almonds in a shallow baking pan and toast, stirring once or twice, until lightly browned and fragrant, about 10 minutes. Cool and then grind (do not pulverize) in a food processor or grinder and set aside.

Butter and flour a baking sheet and shake off excess flour. Mark four 4-inch circles in the floured surface.

Reduce oven heat to 250°F. Beat the egg whites with a pinch of salt until stiff. Gradually add 1 cup of the confectioners' sugar and continue beating until whites hold glossy, firm peaks. Fold in ⅛ teaspoon of the vanilla and the ground almonds. Put the meringue-nut mixture into a pastry bag fitted with a ½-inch plain tip. Pipe meringue in a spiral to fill each circle on the prepared baking sheet.

Bake the meringues immediately in preheated oven until almost dry, about 45 minutes. Cool. Remove meringues from the baking sheet with a wide metal spatula and cool completely in a dry place, such as on a rack in the oven with the heat off. If making ahead, store meringues in an airtight tin (they will go soft in a plastic container).

Meringues can be made a week ahead.

Bring 2 cups of water and the sugar to a simmer in a saucepan and cook until sugar dissolves, about 5 minutes. Add ¼ teaspoon vanilla and the peaches and poach over low heat, carefully turning once or twice, until tender, about 10 minutes. Cool the peaches in their poaching liquid.

Peel, halve, and pit the poached peaches. Cut 1 peach into thin slices.

Recipe can be completed to this point a day ahead.

Whip the cream with the 2 teaspoons sugar and the liqueur until stiff.

Cream can be whipped an hour ahead and refrigerated.

SERVING: Put the meringues on plates. Set a peach half cut side down on top of each meringue. Pipe or spread the chilled whipped cream on top. Top each serving with a few peach slices and sprinkle with a pinch of nutmeg.

YIELD: 4 servings

Montrachet Cheesecake

The slight tang of a mild goat cheese sets off the caramelized pears nicely in this cheesecake.

INGREDIENTS

Cake
5 eggs
2 logs room-temperature Montrachet or other mild chèvre (about 22 ounces)
1¼ cups sugar

Topping
6 dried pear halves
1½ cups vermouth

METHOD

PREPARATION: Bring eggs to room temperature or warm in their shells in hot water. Heat oven to 325°F. Butter and flour a 7-inch cake pan or springform pan. In a bowl, soften cheese with a wooden spoon. Add ½ cup sugar gradually and blend until smooth, or press mixture through a sieve to rid it of any lumps.

In another bowl, whisk together eggs and remaining ¾ cup sugar, incorporating as little air as possible. Stir a small amount of egg mixture into cheese and blend thoroughly. Add remaining egg mixture in small amounts, blending thoroughly after each addition.

Strain entire mixture through a sieve and pour into prepared pan. Place the prepared pan in a larger pan and add water to come halfway up the sides of the cake pan. Bake until top is slightly golden and the cake is just beginning to pull away from the sides of pan, about 1¼ hours. Let cool in pan for 2 hours at room temperature. Invert on a plate or release sides of springform pan and then invert.

Recipe can be made to this point 2 days ahead.

For the topping, in a small saucepan, combine pears, vermouth, and enough water to cover. Bring to a boil and then reduce to a simmer. Cook pears over very low heat until very soft, about 1¼ to 2 hours, depending on moistness of dried fruit. As liquid reduces, continue to add water so that pears are always covered.

Remove pears from liquid and place cut-side down in a small skillet. Add 1 tablespoon of the poaching liquid. Lightly caramelize pears by cooking over high heat for about 5 minutes, taking care not to burn them. For uniform color, spoon liquid over fruit as it cooks. Pears will be very soft. Cool and drain. Arrange pears on top of cheesecake and chill.

Cheesecake can be completed a day ahead.

SERVING: Use a moistened knife to cut cheesecake into wedges.

YIELD: one 7-inch cake

For the Montrachet Cheesecake, caramelize pear halves by cooking for about 5 minutes.

Peggy Cullen
Free-lance writer
New York, NY

Cranberry and Mango Cobbler with Cinnamon and Pecan Cream

This cobbler combines three holiday flavors—cranberry, cinnamon, and pecan—with the surprise tropical flavor of mangoes.

INGREDIENTS

Cinnamon and Pecan Cream, recipe follows

Cobbler Topping
¾ cup flour
½ cup granulated sugar
¼ cup dark-brown sugar
3 ounces butter
Pinch of nutmeg

2 ripe mangoes
6 ounces softened butter
1 cup sugar
1 egg
1½ cups flour
1½ teaspoons baking soda
¾ cup buttermilk
3 cups fresh cranberries

METHOD

PREPARATION: Make the Cinnamon and Pecan Cream. Butter and flour a 9- by 12-inch baking dish.

For the topping, put all ingredients into a bowl and blend until thoroughly combined and crumbly.

Recipe can be made to this point a day ahead.

COOKING AND SERVING: Heat oven to 350°F. Peel mangoes and cut them into cubes. Beat together the butter and ¼ cup of the sugar until light and fluffy. Add the egg and mix. Sift together the flour and baking soda and add alternately with the buttermilk. Spread batter in prepared dish. Toss cranberries and mango cubes with remaining sugar and spread over batter. Sprinkle topping over fruit.

Bake cobbler in preheated oven until browned, about 1 hour and 10 minutes. Let cobbler sit about 15 minutes before serving or serve at room temperature.

Top each serving with Cinnamon and Pecan Cream.

YIELD: 8 servings

Cinnamon and Pecan Cream

INGREDIENTS

5 ounces pecans (1 cup chopped)
1 vanilla bean *or* 1 teaspoon vanilla extract
2 cinnamon sticks
2 cups milk
6 egg yolks
⅔ cup sugar
⅔ cup heavy cream or crème fraîche

METHOD

PREPARATION: Heat oven to 350°F. Spread pecans in a single layer on a shallow baking sheet and toast until browned, about 10 minutes. Cool and chop pecans. If using a vanilla bean, split in half lengthwise, scrape seeds into a large saucepan, and add pod. Break cinnamon sticks into pieces. Add milk, pecans, and cinnamon to saucepan and bring mixture to a boil. Remove from heat and let stand so that flavors infuse, about 30 minutes.

Whisk yolks and sugar together in a large mixing bowl until pale yellow. Bring milk back to a boil. Gradually strain milk into yolk mixture, whisking constantly. Discard flavorings. Return milk mixture to the saucepan. Cook over the lowest possible heat, constantly scraping sides and bottom of pan with a wooden spatula, until custard thickens enough to coat a spoon (160°F), about 10 minutes. If using vanilla extract, add at this point. Pour into a bowl and cool.

Stir in heavy cream or crème fraîche. Cinnamon and Pecan Cream can be made 5 days ahead and refrigerated until ready to use.

YIELD: 3 cups

Stephan Pyles
Chef/co-owner
Routh Street Café
Dallas, TX

Chocolate Truffles

Densely chocolatey, these rich morsels are a perfect after-dinner accompaniment to espresso.

INGREDIENTS

- 4 tablespoons butter
- 10 ounces semisweet chocolate
- 2 egg yolks
- 2 tablespoons confectioners' sugar
- ¼ cup heavy cream

METHOD

PREPARATION: Chop the butter and 6 ounces of the chocolate into small pieces and put in the top of a double boiler set over hot water. Stir frequently until just melted. Remove pan from hot water.

In a small bowl, whisk together the egg yolks, sugar, and cream. Gradually whisk warm chocolate into the eggs. Chill until firm. Grate or shred the remaining 4 ounces of chocolate by hand or in a food processor.

Use 2 teaspoons to divide the chilled mixture into small mounds. Roll the mounds into ¾-inch balls and then roll the balls in the chocolate shreds.

Recipe can be completed several days ahead or can even be frozen.

YIELD: 2 dozen truffles (¾ pound)

Pamela Parseghian
Food editor
COOK'S Magazine

Pineapple Pastry with Caramel Sauce

RICHARD FELBER

Flaky puff pastry encases caramelized pineapples and smooth cream filling in this elegant dessert.

ABOUT PUFF PASTRY

The best puff pastry is tender and flaky, rising up to 5 times its uncooked height. The key to making great puff pastry is to keep the dough cold. Cold, as well as periods of rest, will help prevent the development of gluten in the flour, which makes the dough elastic and, therefore, tough — fine for bread, but not puff pastry. Chill both butter and water. If the weather is hot, you may even want to chill the flour and rolling pin. Over-working the dough also encourages the production of gluten, so work as quickly as possible.

Lindsey Shere
Pastry chef
Chez Panisse
Berkeley, CA

INGREDIENTS

½ **pound Puff Pastry, recipe follows**

Cream Filling
⅓ **cup Pastry Cream (page 136)**
¼ **cup heavy cream**
½ **teaspoon kirsch**

Caramel Sauce
1 **cup water**
¾ **cup sugar**

1 **egg yolk**
1 **tablespoon heavy cream**
½ **fresh pineapple (about ½ pound)**

METHOD

PREPARATION: Make the Puff Pastry. Make the Pastry Cream for the filling, substituting vanilla extract for the liqueur or eau de vie called for in the recipe. Measure ¼ cup of the pastry cream.

Let the pastry dough rest a few minutes on the work surface if the butter is too cold to roll smoothly. On a lightly floured work surface, roll the chilled pastry out to about ⅛ inch thick. Lift the dough gently from the work surface to let it retract so that pieces won't shrink after they've been cut. Cut dough into 3- by 4-inch rectangles or any similar-size shape desired. Put on a baking sheet and chill thoroughly.

For the Caramel Sauce, put ¼ cup of the water in a small saucepan. Add the sugar without stirring. Cook over medium-high heat until golden brown, gently shaking the pan occasionally to prevent uneven cooking, about 5 minutes. Slowly and carefully add remaining ¾ cup water and cook until the caramel dissolves and thickens slightly so that when a small amount is put on a chilled plate it forms a thin syrup, about 5 minutes. Chill.

Mix the egg yolk with 1 tablespoon heavy cream and brush pastry tops. With a knife, cut a ¹⁄₁₆-inch-deep design in the pastry tops, if you like, or cut small designs from scraps of pastry and arrange on top. Refrigerate if not using immediately.

Recipe can be made to this point a day ahead.

Heat oven to 400°F. Bake the pastries in preheated oven for 10 minutes. Lower heat to 350°F and bake until golden and cooked through, about 15 minutes more. Let cool. Carefully split the pastries in half horizontally.

Peel the pineapple, remove the eyes with the tip of a vegetable peeler, quarter, and core. Cut each quarter into ¼-inch-thick slices and then into small wedges.

For the filling, whip the ¼ cup heavy cream and the kirsch together and fold into the chilled Pastry Cream.

Recipe can be completed to this point several hours ahead.

SERVING: In a shallow pan, combine the pineapple wedges and 1 tablespoon of the caramel sauce and warm over low heat.

Spread the bottoms of the pastries with the Cream Filling, place the warm pineapple over it, and set top halves back on. Pour remaining Caramel Sauce around pastries.

YIELD: 4 servings

Puff Pastry

INGREDIENTS

2¾ cups all-purpose flour
1 cup cake flour
1¼ teaspoons salt
1¼ pounds butter

1 lemon
1 cup cold water, approximately

METHOD

PREPARATION: Mix the flours and the salt together in a bowl. Remove ½ cup of the mixture and reserve. Cut 6 ounces of the cold butter into the flour until the mixture has the texture of cornmeal. Squeeze 2 tablespoons lemon juice into a bowl and add 14 tablespoons of water to make 1 cup of liquid. Add water mixture to the flour mixture and toss with a fork to combine. Press together. Do not knead. If necessary, add a bit more water to make a soft dough. Gather the dough into a ball, squeezing to make it hold together, and flatten into a ¾-inch-thick disc. Wrap dough in plastic wrap and refrigerate for 30 minutes.

Meanwhile, beat the remaining 14 ounces of butter with a wooden spoon or rolling pin, or in a mixer, until smooth. Work in the reserved ½ cup of the flour and salt mixture until smooth. The butter should still be cold. Form the butter into a ¾-inch-thick square, wrap in plastic, and refrigerate.

After dough has been chilled at least 30 minutes, roll out on a lightly floured work surface to a ½-inch-thick square. Set the chilled butter diagonally across the center of the square of dough and fold the corners of the dough tightly over the butter as you would the flaps of an envelope, enclosing it completely. Brush off any excess flour and pinch dough to close tightly. Quickly roll this to a ½-inch-thick, 8- by 24-inch rectangle, keeping the corners as square as possible.

Fold the left-hand third of the dough over the center, brush off excess flour, and then fold the right-hand third over, as if you were folding a letter. Rotate the dough 90 degrees. Roll again to a ½-inch, 8- by 24-inch rectangle. Fold in thirds again, wrap in plastic, and chill for 30 minutes.

Roll and fold twice again. Chill the dough for 45 minutes more. Roll and fold the dough two more times and chill the dough at least 2 hours before its final rolling and shaping.

Puff pastry can be made several days ahead, or it can be frozen. Cut off the amount needed and roll and shape as specified.

YIELD: about 2¾ pounds dough

For the Puff Pastry, place the block of butter on the diagonal in the center of the square of pastry dough.

Fold the corners of the dough over the butter as you would the flaps of an envelope.

Roll the dough into a rectangle about twice as long as it is wide.

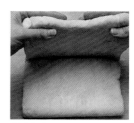

Fold the dough rectangle into thirds as if you were folding a letter.

Chocolate Pots de Crème

An elegant version of chocolate pudding, these pots de crème are creamy and smooth and delicately chocolate flavored.

For the Pots de Crème, skim off any bubbles that form on the surface.

INGREDIENTS

- 2 ounces semisweet chocolate
- 2 cups milk
- 6 egg yolks
- ½ cup sugar
- ½ teaspoon vanilla extract

METHOD

PREPARATION: Heat oven to 325°F. Chop the chocolate into small pieces and put in the top of a double boiler set over hot water. Stir frequently until just melted and remove pan from hot water.

Heat the milk in a small pan over low heat until almost simmering. Remove from heat.

In a bowl, beat the egg yolks with the sugar and vanilla until pale yellow. Gradually stir in the warm chocolate and then the milk. Skim off any bubbles that may have formed on the surface. Gently pour mixture into 2-ounce petits pots or custard cups. Again, skim off any bubbles.

Put in a pan lined with a thin dish towel and carefully pour boiling water around them to come about halfway up the sides. Cover the pots with lids or foil and carefully put into preheated oven. Bake until custard is just set or until a knife inserted in the center comes out clean, about 20 minutes for the pots and 30 minutes for the cups. Remove from water bath. Cool.

Recipe can be completed a day ahead.

SERVING: Serve pots de crème in petits pots or custard cups.

YIELD: 10 pots de crème or 4 to 6 custard cups

Pamela Parseghian
Food editor
COOK'S Magazine

Chocolate Mousse

This dessert is perfect for company and can be made a full day ahead.

INGREDIENTS

½	**pound semisweet chocolate**
4	**eggs**
½	**cup superfine sugar**
¼	**pound softened butter**
2	**tablespoons orange, mint, or other liqueur**
1½	**cups heavy cream, optional**
2	**tablespoons granulated sugar, optional**
¾	**teaspoon vanilla, optional**

METHOD

PREPARATION: Cut the chocolate into small pieces and put in the top of a double boiler set over hot water, stirring frequently until just melted. Remove pan from hot water.

Separate the eggs. Beat the eggs yolks and sugar until pale yellow. Gradually whisk warm chocolate into the yolks to temper them. Gradually beat in the butter and add the liqueur.

Beat the egg whites to stiff peaks. Stir about ¼ of the egg whites into the cooled chocolate mixture and then gently fold in the remaining egg whites.

Transfer mousse to a 1-quart serving dish or four 8-ounce dishes and chill until set, about 2 hours.

Mousse can be completed a day ahead.

Whip the cream with the two tablespoons sugar and vanilla to stiff peaks.

Cream can be whipped an hour ahead.

SERVING: Serve chocolate mousse with whipped cream if desired.

YIELD: 4 servings

Pamela Parseghian
Food editor
COOK'S Magazine

Chocolate Soufflé

ABOUT SOUFFLES

A soufflé rises to such lofty heights thanks to air trapped in the egg whites, which expands when heated. Room-temperature egg whites achieve greater volume. While a balloon whisk and a copper bowl achieve the greatest volume (the albumin in the egg whites reacts chemically with the copper), this can be exhausting and an electric mixer gets fine results. Don't overbeat or overfold the egg whites. Beat the whites just until they maintain glossy peaks.

Fold in the whites, starting by thoroughly mixing in a small amount of white to lighten the base, then quickly folding in the rest. (You should take less than a minute). Don't worry if there are patches of white—better that than overfolding and ending up with a flat soufflé.

Pamela Parseghian
Food editor
COOK'S Magazine

Always a show-stopper, this classic chocolate soufflé is spectacular served plain, but you can serve it with sweetened whipped cream, if you like.

INGREDIENTS

½ cup granulated sugar
5 ounces semisweet chocolate
5 eggs
½ cup heavy cream
2 tablespoons flour
1½ teaspoons vanilla extract
2 tablespoons butter
1½ cups heavy cream, optional
¾ teaspoon vanilla, optional
¼ cup confectioners' sugar

METHOD

PREPARATION: Butter a 1-quart soufflé dish or four 8-ounce soufflé dishes and sprinkle with granulated sugar. Chop chocolate into small pieces. Separate the eggs.

In a small pot, bring the heavy cream and ⅓ cup of the granulated sugar to a boil. Meanwhile, whisk the yolks with the flour and vanilla until light and pale yellow. Add the chocolate bits and butter to the hot cream, remove from heat, and whisk until melted. Gradually whisk warm chocolate mixture into the yolk mixture to temper.

Recipe can be prepared to this point a few hours ahead and kept at room temperature.

Whip the cream with vanilla and 2 tablespoons of the granulated sugar to stiff peaks.

Cream can be whipped an hour ahead.

COOKING AND SERVING: Heat oven to 400°F. Whisk the egg whites until stiff. Gently stir about ¼ of the egg whites into the chocolate mixture; then fold in the remaining whites. Immediately pour the mixture into prepared soufflé dish(es).

Bake soufflé(s) in the center of preheated oven, about 25 minutes for a large soufflé, 10 minutes for smaller ones. Raise heat to 475°F. Put the confectioners' sugar in a sieve. Gently remove soufflé(s) from oven and shake sieve over soufflé(s) to dust with sugar. Return to oven and bake until browned, about 5 minutes more for a large soufflé, 3 minutes more for the smaller ones. Sprinkle again with confectioners' sugar and serve at once with whipped cream if desired.

YIELD: 4 servings

Profiteroles

BILLY ARCE

Classic cream puffs are simple to make and the ideal holder for whipped cream or pastry cream. For profiteroles, they're made small and are floated in chocolate sauce.

INGREDIENTS

Chocolate Sauce
2 tablespoons butter
½ pound semisweet chocolate
¼ cup water
2 tablespoons corn syrup
⅔ cup heavy cream

Pâte à Choux
¾ cup water
¼ pound butter
½ teaspoon salt
1 cup flour
5 eggs

Sweetened Whipped Cream
1½ cups heavy cream
2 tablespoons sugar
¾ teaspoon vanilla extract

METHOD

PREPARATION: *For the Chocolate Sauce,* chop the butter and chocolate into small pieces. Put the butter, chocolate, water, and corn syrup into the top of a double boiler set over hot water. Stir occasionally until chocolate is just melted. Remove from hot water and whisk in cream.

Chocolate Sauce can be made several days ahead.

Line 2 baking pans with parchment paper or butter them and dust with flour.

For the Pâte à Choux, put the water, butter, and salt into a heavy saucepan over medium heat and bring just to a boil. Remove from heat. Add the flour and beat to combine. Return to medium-low heat, stirring constantly and vigorously, until the paste forms a ball and leaves a thin film on the bottom of the pan, about 5 minutes. Remove from heat and let cool for a moment. Add 4 of the eggs, one at a time, beating thoroughly after each addition.

Heat oven to 425°F. Beat the final egg with 1 tablespoon of water for an egg wash. Put the Pâte à Choux into a pastry bag fitted with a ½-inch plain tip. Pipe 1-inch mounds onto the prepared pans, spacing them about 1 inch apart. Or use 2 spoons to form mounds. Lightly brush the tops with the egg wash and bake in preheated oven for 10 minutes. Lower temperature to 350°F and bake until lightly browned and all beads of moisture on the tops have evaporated, about 8 minutes. Cool on a rack in a dry place.

Recipe can be made to this point a few hours ahead.

Whip the heavy cream with the sugar and vanilla extract until just stiff.

The cream can be whipped an hour ahead.

SERVING: Bring the Chocolate Sauce back to room temperature if refrigerated. Put the whipped cream into a pastry bag fitted with a ½-inch fluted tip. With a serrated or sharp paring knife, cut the tops off the pastry puffs and pipe or spoon in the cream. Replace the tops.

Pour some Chocolate Sauce onto each plate. Put the cream puffs on top of sauce and serve at once.

YIELD: 4 servings

For the profiteroles, *cook until the dough forms a ball and a thin film forms on the bottom of the pan, about 5 minutes.*

Add the eggs one by one. Make a deep indentation in the dough and drop egg into it.

Pamela Parseghian
Food editor
COOK'S Magazine

Index